Meditations *at* Twilight *on* Genesis

Meditations *at* Twilight *on* Genesis

Rabbi
Melvin Granatstein

Urim Publications
Jerusalem • New York

Meditations at Twilight on Genesis
by Melvin Granatstein

Typeset by Ariel Walden

Printed in Israel

First Edition

ISBN 978-965-524-167-9

Urim Publications, P.O. Box 52287,
Jerusalem 9152102 Israel

www.UrimPublications.com

Library of Congress Cataloging-in-Publication Data

Granatstein, Melvin, author.
Meditations at twilight on Genesis / Rabbi Melvin Granatstein.
pages cm
ISBN 978-965-524-167-9 (hardback)
1. Bible. Genesis--Commentaries. I. Title.
BS1235.53.G73 2015
222'.1107--dc23 2014050116

Donor List

Thank you to the following contributors whose generosity enabled this collection of essays.

Dr. Mark and Nancy Aeder
Rabbi Yehuda and Hannah Appel
Dr. David Bar Shain
Barbara Baskin
Dr. Jonathan and Dahna Baskin
Dr. Joseph and Dr. Revital Baskin
Philip Baskin
Dr. Yehuda Baskin
Irving Berliner
Nathan Berliner
Dr. George and Helene Bernstein
Dr. Hillel Chiel and Dr. Elizabeth Dreben
Carl and Shirley Cohen
Gary and Zippora Coleman
Dan *(z"l)* and Leigh Cord
Diana Davis
Leonard and Karen Ehrenreich
Eitan Flank
Eva Freireich
Amy and Jordan Gorfinkel
Pearl and Albert Hersh
Dr. Avi Jacobs
Ari Jaffe
Dr. Jack Jaffe
Rabbi Avery and Aliza Joel
Dr. Daniel and Esther Kahn
Miriam Katz
Judy Kirchick
Steve and Sandy LassersonJordan and Jane Lefko
Josh and Illana Mandel
Golda Mayers
Alice Mendlovic
Joseph Moskowitz
Dr. Sigmund and Nadene Norr
Carol and David Paley
C. H. Raskind
Joseph and Sarah Rudolph
Karol *(z"l)* and Joan Saks
Dr. David and Mila Schwam
Dr. Jeffrey and Lesley Schwersenski
Dr. David and Dr. Tamar Shafran
Joseph Shafran
Boaz Shevach
Dr. Thelma Silver
Dr. Alan and Rivka Spiegel
Igor and Tatyana Spira
Dr. Joshua and Elizabeth Sunshine
Dr. Ira and Barbara Taub
Harvey and Edith Tesler
Dr. Philip Toltzis
Albert and Cynthia Uvlin
Dr. Stanley and Doreen Warn
Martin Weisberg
Dr. Michael Wolf
Regina Wolovitz
Issac Zemelman

To Malka
In All Seasons
My Beloved Companion

Contents

Introduction

THE FIVE BOOKS OF THE TORAH constitute the primary canonical text of Judaism, and for that reason, the annual reading of the entire Torah during the morning Shabbat service is central to that service. But this ancient text is brought to life for traditional Judaism by being read within a context that embraces the rest of the canonical books of Hebrew scripture – the Tanakh, the fundamental canon of the Oral Torah collected in the Talmud and the contemporaneous works of the Midrash, along with the vast array of Jewish thought and religious literature down to our day.

No one can read any text without bringing to bear his or her own baggage of personal and cultural assumptions. When reading so ancient a work as the Torah, it is important to read that work with sensitivity to the cultural and linguistic environment in which it was written. In this collection of essays on *Sefer B'reishit*, or Book of Genesis, I have attempted to make myself aware of that cultural environment and to be sensitive to it. However, I make no apologies for writing as a contemporary Jew steeped in the classical tradition of *parshanut*, or Jewish literary exegesis.

Let me address my motivation in writing one more study of *Sefer B'reishit*. For 37 years, I had the good fortune to serve as the Rav of the Green Road Synagogue – Shearit HaP'leata B'nai Ya'acov in Beachwood, Ohio. Each Shabbat, as the day drew to a close and we would celebrate the concluding Shabbat at *se'udat sh'lishit*, or the third Shabbat meal, I had the honor of meditating aloud upon the weekly Torah *parasha* to a receptive audience of men and women of diverse ages and backgrounds – hence the title, *"Meditations at Twilight"* – and over these many years, listeners would urge me to publish at least some of these cogitations. I have focused upon those *Divrei Torah* that are primarily concerned with what I believe is the plain meaning of the text – what we refer to as *p'shat*. Ultimately, it is the *p'shat* that can most profoundly reveal the great moral and spiritual truths of Judaism.

The plain meaning of the text is not the same as the literal meaning of the words. The Torah is rich in imaginative narrative and metaphorical evocations whose meanings must be deciphered by the careful reader. Just consider these striking words of the *Zohar*.

> Woe to the one who says that the Torah comes to present ordinary stories and the observations of ordinary people . . . Rather, all of the words of the Torah are of exalted matters and supernal mysteries . . . The Torah has a body – these are the Torah's commandments. . . . This body is clothed in garments, which are worldly narratives. Ordinary fools only look at the garments, the narrative, and see nothing else, not seeing what lies beneath the garments. Those who know more focus not only on the garments, but on the body which is concealed beneath the garments. But the wise servants of the King who stood at Sinai peer at [the Torah's] soul. (*Zohar* III 152a)

It is here that traditional exegesis, *parshanut*, is especially insightful, and I have mined this literature for its penetrating wisdom. The Talmud, the great Midrashic classics such as *B'reishit Rabba*, *Pirkei de Rabbi Eliezer*, and *Midrash Tanhuma*; classic works of Jewish philosophic thought such as Rambam's *Moreh Nevukhim* and the *Zohar*; the commentaries of such luminaries as Rashi, Ibn Ezra, and Ramban among others, serve as powerful sources for understanding the soul of the Torah text. I have used these sources while not ignoring more recent commentaries and modern scholarship with the hope of informing the reader's understanding of the basic Torah text.

The sages tell us that there are "seventy facets to the Torah" or, as we might say, that the Torah admits to multiple layers of meaning. Rabbi Isaac Luria, the great sixteenth century mystic and Kabbalist remarked that just as 600,000 Israelites stood at Sinai to receive the Torah and there are 600,000 letters in the Torah, each Israelite possesses his own letter, which serves as a point of orientation for understanding all of the other letters. No dogmatic claim is being made to finality in this book. To the contrary, if these essays evoke a desire to explore the Torah freshly, from the perspective of one's own letter, so to speak, this collection will have served its purpose.

A word about method. While I have usually used the JPS translation of the Torah, from time to time I have dissented and translated verses according to my own understanding. In my use of the classical commentaries, wherever possible I have relied upon the superb version of the *Mikraot Gedolot, Torat Hayim* published by Mosad HaRav Kook. I have attempted to keep footnotes at a minimum, referencing classical sources within the text itself.

While many urged me to publish, there are many good friends I especially want to thank. I first want to express my debt to my beloved friend, the late Dr. Shmuel Spero, of blessed memory, whose dazzling spiritual presence and constant encouragement was decisive. "*Lehavdil bein hayim lehayim,*" I must profoundly thank Benjamin Baskin, a gabbai in our synagogue and a wonderful friend who, singlehandedly and at his own initiative, became the effective manager of this project and an energetic promoter of the entire endeavor. This work would not have been possible without his encouragement and support. In addition to his technical help, Ben was an insightful reader of many of these essays, sharpening my presentation. I cannot thank him enough.

Adena Muskin, a talented and dedicated young woman, served as my typist and computer "maven," bringing many useful insights of her own to this work.

A special thanks to Dr. Hillel Chiel and to my son-in-law, Dr. Oren Meyers, for reading some of the early essays and offering useful suggestions. I am especially grateful to Dr. Moshe Sokolow, an academic scholar of Bible at Yeshiva University, who meticulously read each essay and astutely commented and offered important criticism, which helped immensely in preparing this work for publication.

I would be remiss if I did not thank the many generous contributors who provided the financial underpinnings of this project, and I have included an honor list of these friends.

Aharona, aharona haviva, I thank my wife Malka to whom this volume is dedicated. She is my partner in all of my endeavors, and she read these essays as they were being composed. As always, her comments were incisive and vital.

Finally, I praise the God of Israel who has allowed me to be among those who dwell in the Beit Midrash of Torah. I can do no better than to cite the verse from the Psalms cited by the *Zohar* in the passage quoted above:

> גַּל עֵינַי וְאַבִּיטָה נִפְלָאוֹת מִתּוֹרָתֶךָ
>
> Open my eyes that I might see wonders from Your Torah. (Psalms 119:18)

Chapter 1

Creation and Nothingness

PARASHAT B'REISHIT

When the Torah begins its narrative of God's creation of heaven and earth, it employs the Hebrew word ברא – *bara,* for "created." The Midrash *B'reishit Rabba* (*Parashat B'reishit* 1:8) recounts that a philosopher once said to Rabban Gamliel: "Your God is a great craftsman but he found wonderful ingredients to help him: *tohu, bohu,* the dark, the wind, the water, the depths." Rabban Gamliel angrily dismissed this philosopher's comment, asserting that each of those ingredients was itself created. The critical term ברא – *bara* is used here, and verses are cited to prove that God created each of those items. But this merely pushes the philosopher's assertion back one step. What this person asserted is that God created the world out of some kind of preexistent raw material. If these ingredients were themselves created, out of which material were *they* created?

Following an ancient tradition undoubtedly reflected in this Midrash, Ramban insists that the term ברא – *bara* – means creation מאפיסה מוחלטת, "out of absolute nothingness" (Commentary on *B'reishit* 1:1). Using the scholastic Latin term, God fashions the world *creatio ex nihilo.*

But what does this mean? Absolute nothingness is incomprehensible.[1] Tentatively, we might say that it means that God

1. In this regard see Henri Bergson, *Creative Evolution* (Modern Library), 296–324. See also Jean Paul Satre, *Being and Nothingness* (Washington Square Press), 33–85.

creates the world out of nothing other than his own being.[2] But since we cannot know God's being – "no man can see the face of God and live" – it is not clear that this assertion is saying anything at all.

Ibn Ezra dismisses the notion that the critical term ברא – *bara* means *creatio ex nihilo*. He cites a number of biblical verses in which the term ברא – *bara* is used but clearly means creation out of something. For example, on the fourth day of Creation the Torah says: וַיִּבְרָא אֱ-לֹהִים אֶת הַתַּנִּינִם הַגְּדֹלִים – "God *created* the great sea monsters" (*B'reishit* 1:21), but it is clear from the context that these creatures are fashioned out of the sea.

In *Sefer Bamidbar* when the Torah records the rebellion of Korah, Moses tells the people that the rebels will be swallowed up by the earth, and he introduces this by saying: וְאִם בְּרִיאָה יִבְרָא ה'. Using the critical term ברא – *bara* he is saying, "But if God brings about something unheard of" (*Bamidbar* 16:30, JPS translation). By no account can *creatio ex nihilo* be intended here. Other striking examples are cited by Ibn Ezra (Commentary on *B'reishit* 1:1).

This leads Ibn Ezra to define this term very differently. ברא – *bara* means to divide or to slice. For example, Ezekiel 23:47 says: וּבָרֵא אוֹתְהֶן בְּחַרְבוֹתָם – "They will *slice* them with their swords." In the context of the Creation narrative, God divides, slices out, or in more appropriate terminology, draws lines and defines – determines the boundaries of – heaven and earth. To create is to cut out, shape, and define. Ibn Ezra reads the first verse of the Torah much the way JPS reads it: "When God began to create the heaven and the earth – the earth being *unformed* and *void* – *tohu* and *bohu*." Where there is initially only empty chaos, God defines order. It must be admitted that this sounds like the philosopher so angrily denounced by Rabban Gamliel in the Midrash.

2. Creation out of nothing in this sense is, in fact, a fundamental notion found in Kabbala. But this is different from מאפיסה מוחלטת, as stated here in Ramban. In this Kabbalistic doctrine, אין emerges from אי"ן סוף, or God's infinitude. See Gershom-Scholem, *Major Trends in Jewish Mysticism* (Schoken Publishing House, 1941) 25. See also שערי אורה לרבינו יוסף גיקטיליא Y. Boker ed. (Jerusalem, 1965), 408.

But Ibn Ezra in his commentary is making a point not found in the brief comments of the philosopher of the Midrash. Creation is a process of delineating ever more progressive distinctions. Thus God defines heaven and earth, then separates the light from the darkness, the upper waters from the lower waters, the sea from the land, and fashions all of the forms of life as distinct and separate species. Where the primal chaos comes from is simply not addressed by the Torah's Creation story.

No less a champion of Rabbinic Orthodoxy than the Gaon of Vilna denies that ברא – *bara* necessarily means *creatio ex nihilo*. Closely mirroring the arguments of Ibn Ezra, citing many of the same verses, the Gaon draws our attention to three distinct terms used in the creation story: ברא, *bara* –"creates"; יצר, *yatsar* – "forms"; עשה, *asa* – "makes." In this rendering, "creates" applies to "substances" only God can fashion even if fashioned out of something preexistent. "Forms" refers to items that are measurable. "Makes" refers to the perfection of items.[3]

The *Yotser* blessing recited each morning in the morning service begins with a slightly modified verse from Isaiah 45:7: יוֹצֵר אוֹר וּבוֹרֵא חֹשֶׁךְ עֹשֶׂה שָׁלוֹם וּבוֹרֵא רָע – "[God] *forms* the light and *creates* darkness, *makes* peace and *creates* evil." The Gaon says that the light is "formed" because it is a measurable substance cast against darkness that is immeasurable. The darkness is "created." But on the other hand, God "makes" peace repairing and perfecting his world. He "creates" evil, which, like darkness, is immeasurable and irreducible. Darkness and evil may well be described as the absence of light and peace, but they are irreducible nonetheless and altogether real in human experience.

There is perhaps another way to understand the term ברא – *bara* or "create." The Mishna in *Avot* (5:1) tells us: "With ten pronouncements was the world created." The Mishna reflects upon the fact that in the Torah's account, Creation proceeds with God's verbal commands. "God *said*, 'Let there be light,' and there is light" (*B'reishit* 1:3). Every item of Creation cited in the first chapter of *B'reishit* is called into existence through God's word. "He spoke and it happened; He commanded and

3. אדרת אליהו Meir Yechiel Halter, ed. (Warsaw) 1884, Vol. I, 14–15.

it emerged" (Psalms 148:5). Building upon the straightforward assertion that Creation emerges from God's words, the ancient text *Sefer Yetsira* makes the astonishing assertion that God forms the items of Creation from combinations of the letters of the Hebrew alphabet.[4] But this has the unavoidable implication of saying that God creates his world out of his words. The letters of the alphabet are, so to speak, the atoms of language, the elements out of which words are formed.

Human beings think and articulate their thoughts through language. Language, human speech, is the instrument through which we can comprehend our world, which is God's creation. The structure of the world is the handiwork of God and insofar as we comprehend that structure we can read the mind of God. Galileo said that the universe is God's book and if we "read" that book we know God's thoughts.

The assertion of *Sefer Yetsira* that God creates the world through proper combination of letters, the atoms of words, thought, and articulation, means that God creates whatever exists through His thoughts.[5] It further means that through language, we have the tools to connect to God as Creator. As is well known, Rambam insists that studying the laws of nature is the way to the knowledge of God (see especially *Moreh Nevukhim* III, 51).

If whatever exists, exists only through the articulation of God's thoughts, this of necessity will include the "ingredients" that the Midrash's philosopher imagined that God needed for Creation. Perhaps, this doctrine of *Sefer Yetsira* can provide us with a means to talk about the notion of *creatio ex nihilo*. The world emerges from nothing other than the articulation of God's thoughts.

Targum Yerushalmi, one of the Aramaic translations of the Torah reaching us from early medieval times, translates the first three words of the Torah: בחוכמא ברא ה', "with wisdom did God create." The identification of the beginning of Creation with

4. *Sefer Yetsira*, Lewin Epstein (Jerusalem, 1965). See Chapter 1, Mishna 1; Chapter 3, Mishna 3–5 (in נוסחא א)

5. With this notion, *Sefer Yetsira* antedates the theories of Bishop G. Berkeley by at least 1,400 years.

Divine wisdom is a persistent theme in Jewish thought, especially with regard to the Creation story. It also neatly fits with *Sefer Yetsira*'s insight that Creation is the articulation of God's thoughts or his wisdom.

We are told in Proverbs (8:22) that wisdom was created before the creation of the world and that wisdom was God's אמון – *amon* (8:30). This term אמון – *amon* has been variously translated as confidant, student, or craftsman's tool. Following the latter translation, the Midrash *B'reishit Rabba* compares Divine wisdom to an architect's blueprint (*Parashat B'reishit* 1:1). Furthermore, this Midrash identifies Divine wisdom both with the marvels of creation as well as with the Torah, and states remarkably: "Thus the Holy One, blessed be he, looked into the Torah and created the world."

Nothing can rob such Midrashim of meaning more than misplaced literalism. Clearly the Rabbis did not imagine that there was a giant Sefer Torah in the sky that God consulted. Rather, the Rabbis believed that Divine wisdom, whether expressed in the wonders of the universe or in the words and letters of the Torah, were all of one piece. God's unitary wisdom can be found in both. And wisdom is the beginning of everything.

All of this suggests that once we have reconsidered *creatio ex nihilo*, we can think of it as the emergence of Creation out of nothing *other than God's thoughts*. Once we have identified the beginning of everything with God's wisdom, we have freed the Hebrew word ברא – *bara* from the iron constraints of exclusively meaning *creatio ex nihilo*. God creates heaven and earth through the articulation of His thoughts. However, when He created the great sea monsters on day four of Creation, He presumably uses materials already called into existence. If so, Ibn Ezra's definition of ברא – *bara* as the defining of boundaries is altogether plausible. So "at the beginning of the articulation of God's wisdom (Targum Yerushalmi's rendering of the first three words of the Torah) God creates heaven and earth." And according to Ibn Ezra, he does so by defining their boundaries.

In fact, the process of Creation on the first six days involves progressive differentiation. Well known is the Midrash that says that these six days can be grouped in pairs. This is usually understood to mean that day one finds its pair in day two, day three with day four, day five with day six (*B'reishit Rabba* 11:8). In the *Zohar*, a far more striking process of pairing is presented. Here day one, on which light was created, is paired with day four, on which the *lights* – the sun, moon and stars – are created. Day two, on which the sky and sea are created, is paired with day five, on which the species of fowl and fish that occupy the sky and sea are created. Day three, on which the dry land is created, is paired with day six, on which land animals and man are created. In each pair, the second day of the unit transforms the simple element of the first into differentiated parts (*Zohar* III 219b). The *Zohar*'s identification of this pattern lays bare the theme of Creation that moves from the formless to the complex, structured world in which man is to serve his Creator.

Chapter 2

Artistry, Goodness, and the Image of God

PARASHAT B'REISHIT

"THE TORAH SPEAKS in the language of men." What was originally an exegetical rule of the Beit Midrash of Rabbi Ishmael becomes, in Rambam's hands, an appeal for nuanced, sensitive reading of biblical texts. Misplaced literalism and a deafness to metaphor and symbol have not only led to unnecessary rejections of the indisputable claims of modern evolutionary biology, but have also rendered us insensitive to the beauty and wisdom of the Torah's Creation narrative.

The Talmud in Tractate *Megilla* 14a, playing on a verse from Hanna's prayer in the Book of Samuel exclaims, וְאֵין צוּר כֵּא־לֹהֵינוּ – "There is no צייר, craftsman, like our God."

Consider the first chapter in *B'reishit*. God calls the elements of Creation into existence and with each new creation, the Torah tells us that וַיַּרְא אֱ־לֹהִים כִּי־טוֹב – "God saw that it was good." What is this like? It is like an artist who paints upon a canvas. He then steps back to contemplate his work, finds it satisfying, and says that it is good.[6] He then proceeds to the next step of his work in

6. Of all people, it was John Dewey who pointed this out in *Art as Experience* (Capricorn Books, 1958), 49: "The process of art in production is related to the aesthetic in perception organically, as the Lord God in creation surveyed His work and found it good." Also on page 65: "... the expression of the self in and through a medium constituting the work of art is itself a prolonged interaction of something issuing from the self ... Even the Almighty took seven days to create

progress. God sees that "it was good" at each point. This occurs seven times in the first Creation narrative. On day six, as the Shabbat is about to arrive, the Torah tells us, וַיַּרְא אֱ־לֹהִים אֶת כָּל־אֲשֶׁר עָשָׂה וְהִנֵּה־טוֹב מְאֹד – "God saw all that he had made and it was very good" (*B'reishit* 1:31).

The divine Artist has completed His work and He is fully satisfied. The sixth and final day has ended; the seventh day, Shabbat – literally the "Day of Cessation" – begins. God "ceases all the work He has done on day seven. He blesses the day and 'sanctifies' it" or sets it apart (*B'reishit* 2:2–3).

Now in this masterwork of the great Artist, there is one item of His oevre that God studiously avoids pronouncing good.[7] That item is the human being. This cannot be because man is unimportant. Anyone with a feeling for Biblical Hebrew cannot help noting the mounting excitement in the language that announces the human being's immanent creation. Indeed we are told that man is to be fashioned in God's image and to be made master of all the creatures already called into existence. When the Torah concludes the account of man's creation, the prose of the text transitions into poetic cadence:

> וַיִּבְרָא אֱ־לֹהִים אֶת הָאָדָם בְּצַלְמוֹ בְּצֶלֶם אֱ־לֹהִים בָּרָא אֹתוֹ זָכָר וּנְקֵבָה בָּרָא אֹתָם
> God created man in His image, in the image of God did He create him, male and female He created them. (*B'reishit* 1:27)

Why should the centerpiece of God's artwork be treated with such reserve that God refuses to call it good? The answer will come not in any explicit statement of the Torah, but will be made clear as the human being's story begins to unfold. Whether the creation of man is a good thing or not can only be decided by

---

the heaven and the earth . . . and it was only at the end of that period that He was aware of just what He set out to do with the raw material of chaos that confronted him." My attention was drawn to this reference in a discussion with Rabbi Shubert Spero.

7. To be sure, on day two the word "good" is not pronounced. This is because the item created, namely the water, is completed only on day three, and there indeed the Torah employs the term "good."

man himself. It will be determined by the human being's freely chosen decisions.

This must be the case, because man has been created in the image of the great Artist. Works of art only emerge out of the free choices of the artist. This creature, created in God's image, possesses an analogous capacity for free choice. The choices made by this centerpiece of the great artwork of Creation will prove fateful. Whether the beautiful canvas painted by the great Artist will retain its beauty or be altogether spoiled will be determined by the decisions of the central item on the canvas.

At the end of *Parashat B'reishit*, judgment will be rendered. There the Torah will tell us that God once more will contemplate his artistry. וַיַּרְא ה' – "God sees." But what God will see is כִּי רַבָּה רָעַת הָאָדָם בָּאָרֶץ – ". . . great is the evil of man upon the earth." וַיִּתְעַצֵּב אֶל לִבּוֹ – God is heartsick. He says אֶמְחֶה – "I will *erase* the human being I have created" together with all other creatures because, as God says, "I regret that I made them" (*B'reishit* 6:5–8).

Of course that will not be the end of the story, because "Noah finds favor" in God's eyes. But God will nonetheless erase most of the lines of heaven and earth and begin his artwork again after the great flood. But we are getting ahead of ourselves. As Rashi already notes (Commentary on 2:8), there are not one but two Creation stories: the first story details the seven days of Creation, while the second account focuses upon man as the centerpiece of God's Creation. Here God fashions man out of the dust of the earth while breathing the breath of life into his nostrils.[8] Again it is Rashi who observes that this means that human consciousness, and therefore the possibilities of moral choice, can embrace the greatest heights or the deepest depravity (2:7).

The Torah tells us that God "breathed the breath of life into man's nostrils" and man became a נֶפֶשׁ חַיָּה – a "living being" (2:7). Onkeles translates "living being" as רוח ממללא – "a speaking spirit." Man's power of speech will be critical as the narrative of the first man continues. God will now bring each creature that

8. In his magisterial essay, "The Lonely Man of Faith," *Tradition* 1965, Rabbi Joseph B. Soloveitchik expands on the polar tension in the separate accounts of man's creation.

he fashions before man to see what name man will assign to it. The name that man assigns to each creature will be canonized by God (2:19).

Just as God fashioned all the elements of Creation by calling them into existence, so too will man, fashioned in God's image, name them and classify them through the power of speech. God orders his creation through the articulation of his commands, and man will order his raw experience of God's world through his power of articulation. It is partially in this sense that in the terminology of the Talmud, man is God's partner in Creation (*Shabbat* 10a).

Now this power to speak and articulate, think and organize makes man unique among all of the creatures of the earth. But uniqueness comes at a price. As the Torah tells us, what man discovers as he organizes the world of his experience is that he is alone. He can find no companion among the creatures that he names. If the human being is to find a coequal helpmate, he will have to look to himself with the help of God.

In *B'reishit* 1:27, when God creates man, the Torah tells us זָכָר וּנְקֵבָה בָּרָא אֹתָם – "male and female did He create them." But in the second Creation account of *B'reishit*, man is said to be initially alone. When this man becomes aware of his loneliness, God renders the judgment that it is not good for him to be alone. God then casts man into a deep sleep and takes one of his צלעות – *tsla'ot* and fashions a woman from it. In standard translations both ancient and modern, צלע – *tsela* is translated as "rib." Indeed the Targum Yonatan, following one Midrashic tradition, goes so far as to specify that woman was created from the thirteenth rib on the right side of the man.

However, in several places in the Talmud and in Midrash *B'reishit Rabba* the word "*tsela*" is rendered not as "rib" but as "side." Indeed there are good biblical precedents for translating "*tsela*" as "side." For example, in *Sh'mot* 26 this term is used for the sides of the Mishkan, or desert sanctuary. These rabbinic sources understand this passage in *B'reishit* to mean that God creates woman from one of the man's sides.

The question here is what does "man's side" mean? Rashi, following ample rabbinic antecedents, comments on *B'reishit*

1:27 that the human being was initially formed דו־פרצופים – with two facets: a masculine persona and a feminine persona. In a word, the human being was created as an androgyne. This has the advantage of explaining the sense in which the human being was created as both male and female in *B'reishit* 1:27. In this rendering then, woman was fashioned from the feminine facet of the human being.

When the male awakes from his sleep and finds his female counterpart as a separate being, he exclaims, "At last, this one is bone of my bone and flesh of my flesh. She shall be called אִשָּׁה – woman, כִּי מֵאִישׁ לֻקְחָה זֹּאת – "for she was taken from man." The Torah then editorializes, "Therefore shall a man leave his father and his mother and cling to his wife so that they become one flesh." But woman has just been separated from man. The androgynous state that prevailed before the great sleep was cast upon man is now irrevocably broken. Before the sleep, man and woman were physically of "one flesh." In what special sense will man and woman become "one flesh" now that they are separated?

Rashi avers that husband and wife become one flesh in their offspring (Commentary on *B'reishit* 1:24). But here Ramban objects. After all, male and female of every species will become one flesh in their children, if what is meant by that term is merely sexual reproduction. But the Torah seems to be describing a uniquely human relationship. Ramban insists that the key term here is וְדָבַק בְּאִשְׁתּוֹ – "he shall cling to his wife." What is characteristically human is our ability to create attachments to a spouse so profound that we seek to cling to that person and be always with them. Our love for our spouse transcends our love for our parents, whom we leave behind in order to fuse our beings with him or her. It is in this new sense that we become one flesh, not physically, but emotionally, and in spirit (Commentary ad locum).

It should be clear that the Torah is portraying the human condition in metaphorical terms. The human being created in God's image is not male alone or female alone, but male and female taken together. Man alone or woman alone is incomplete. When a man and woman find each other in the context of marital love, they are recapturing the image of God within themselves. This then is what the Torah means when it says that man and woman become "one flesh." Ramban explains this as the outcome of the unique way a human husband and wife "cling" to each other.

Using the same set of symbols – the androgynous beginning of the human being, the severing of the male and female from each other, and their reunion in marriage – the *Zohar* (II 44b) provides us with the following account. The original male and female persona were attached "side by side" at the back so that they could not see each other face to face. God separates these persona to enable them to look at each other, to embrace each other, and uniquely among animals, have sexual relations encountering each other fully as persons face to face.[9] The *Zohar* describes the event with the following account:

> What does "one of his sides" (*B'reishit* 2:21) mean? This refers to the female side. "He brings her to the man." This means He adorns her as a bride and presents her to the man. With glowing faces they behold each other.

Now the human being can conquer his loneliness in a face-to-face encounter that makes man and woman one flesh in the sense intended by Ramban. In other words, "one flesh" refers to the marital relationship and the sense of wholeness and integrity it brings.

The Torah will now digress and tell the story of the fateful events that will befall the human couple in the Garden of Eden. But after that, the Torah will resume the account that began with man being charged to name all of the other species. It was in that context that man found himself utterly alone and lonely. Woman was then fashioned from the female side of his body so

9. The Talmud, Tractate *Bekhorot* 8a, says that three creatures engage sexually face-to-face: the human, the snake, and the fish. This comment is thought to be alluding to some esoteric mystery. For our purposes, we should note that the snake becomes a symbol of the "evil inclination" or raw instinct. The fish comes to symbolize the hidden within the human psyche.

that he might find a companion worthy and equal to himself.

This story is brought to its climax after man's expulsion from the Garden of Eden. Returning to his task of naming all creatures, the man will now name "his" woman, Hava, which the Torah says, means "the mother of all who live."

Chapter 3

Knowledge, Life, and Temptation

PARASHAT B'REISHIT

THE STORY OF MAN in the Garden of Eden (Adam and Eve in the standard English transliterations) cries out for interpretation. The Hebrew term "*eden*" means pleasure and this pleasure garden contains a tree of life and a tree of the knowledge of good and bad. The human being is placed in this garden to work and tend it, and is given free rein to enjoy its fruits – with one exception. Adam is forbidden to eat from the tree of knowledge of good and bad, and is forewarned that if he violates this prohibition, on that day he will die (*B'reishit* 2:8–18).

We are further told that the man and his wife were naked and, nonetheless, without a sense of shame. The snake, which is "the most cunning of all the creatures God has made" (*B'reishit* 3:1) – a symbol of temptation and wickedness – tempts the woman to take the forbidden fruit and eat it. He tells her that the sole reason God has prohibited this tree's fruit to her husband and to her is in order to prevent them from knowing what God knows and thus becoming godlike. Eve then takes the fruit, eats it, and shares it with her husband. Their eyes are indeed opened and the great information they now receive is that they are naked – knowledge that now fills them with shame (*B'reishit* 2:25–3:7).

The commentators have provided us with a plethora of explanations for this narrative. Let us consider just a few.

One question seems to ask itself. Why would God forbid

knowledge to the human being created in his image? Rambam, who asserts that the image of God in man refers to the human capacity to think and reason, raises the above question in the second chapter of his great philosophical work (*Moreh Nevukhim* I 1–2). He then sets down his understanding of the story. For Rambam, the tree of life symbolizes truth about life and general existence, or simply, the difference between truth and falsehood. The tree of the knowledge of the good and bad symbolizes the awareness of the pleasant and the unpleasant, pleasure and its absence. Its fruit focuses our attention upon the ephemeral.

As long as man stayed focused upon truth and the distinction between truth and falsehood, the naked condition of his body was of no importance to him. The mortal sin of Adam and Eve was to turn away from objective truth – מושכלות – to focus upon subjective appearance and pleasure – מפורסמות. This is what brought shame into the world. Arguably, what Rambam seeks to do in his philosophic work *Moreh Nevukhim* is to plot the steps that will lead us away from the superficial focus upon appearance and pleasure, and refocus our minds and spirit on the search for truth, or the tree of life.

Ibn Ezra understands the elements of this story differently (Commentary on *B'reishit* 2:25). For him, the story is principally a parable about sexual awakening. The forbidden fruit of sexual awareness is what leads to shame. But why should sexual awakening in creatures fashioned as sexual beings, and who are sexually differentiated into male and female, be initially forbidden? A shrewder focus upon the account of man's nakedness is presented by Rabbi Ovadia Seforno who argues that in the initial innocence of man, sexuality could be enjoyed as the fulfillment of God's purpose without shame. Something else apart from sex must have intruded into human consciousness to make human beings ashamed (Commentary on *B'reishit* 2:25).

Ramban cites Ibn Ezra's comments but, like Seforno, denies that the fruit of the tree of knowledge induced mere sexual desire. Rather, Ramban asserts that prior to eating from the forbidden tree, the human being acted without desire or will, but merely out of necessity to do the will of God. What the fruit of this tree did was to initiate in man desire and choice, which in turn introduced the possibility of moral evil and the shame that comes from moral failure (Commentary on *B'reishit* 2:9).

This interpretation has filled students of Ramban's commentary with consternation. Firstly, if prior to the sin of the forbidden fruit human beings acted only out of necessity in God's service, what made the decision to disobey God possible? Secondly, this means that the exercise of free will and human autonomy is undesirable, something that flies in the face of conventional understandings of Judaism.

In fact, Ramban offers us an alternative way to understand the Garden narrative, not in his commentary on *B'reishit* but in his commentary on *Vayikra, Parashat Emor* 23:40–41. There the Torah introduces the mitsvah of the four species for the festival of Succot (taking up the palm branch and citron, myrtles and willows). In this observance we hold the palm branch, myrtles, and willows tied together in our right hand and hold the citron in our left, and we then place it adjacent to the bundled species. Ramban, following mystical sources, identifies the citron with the fruit of the tree of knowledge.

To better understand the full implications of Ramban's treatment of the mitsvah of the four species with reference to the Garden story in *B'reishit*, we must turn to the *Zohar* (I 221). The *Zohar* tells us that God wanted man to cleave to Him with a singular heart at a unitary place where nothing changes. This, the *Zohar* tells us, refers to the tree of life. But with the sin of eating the fruit of the tree of knowledge, man abandoned the unitary tree of life in order to cleave to a place where everything changes – from good to evil and from evil to good. At that moment, the tree of knowledge was cut away from the unitary tree of life, introducing disintegration into our world and into our consciousness. This is the beginning of idolatry with its multiplicity of gods, mirroring the multifaceted, disjointed nature of the world of our consciousness.

Following this reconstruction of the Garden of Eden story, Ramban understands the mitsvah of the four species to be an enactment of symbolic repair of our disintegrated world and consciousness, as we restore the citron, the fruit of the tree of knowledge, into a unitary framework with the other species representing the wholeness of God's Creation.

In a very different mode of interpretation, the modern scholar Moshe David Cassuto places his focus upon God's warning that "on the day" man eats from the tree of knowledge, he will die. But in fact, Adam lives 930 years!

The knowledge proffered by the forbidden tree, according to Cassuto, is the knowledge that man is mortal.[10] On the very day man discovers the fact of his mortality, death-consciousness becomes all-pervasive for him and changes everything. Ipso facto, man is expelled from the pleasant garden of the tree of life and cast into a frightening, threatening world in which he knows his nakedness and vulnerability. His genitals testify to his mortality. The only immortality possible in this world will come through sexual reproduction.

This interpretation has the advantage of clarifying the real significance of the curse imposed upon the snake, the woman, and the man in *B'reishit* 3:14–20. Eternal enmity will now prevail between man and the snake, which now represents the threatening character of untamed nature.[11] Woman will assure her immortality only through the pain of childbirth. To protect both herself and her children, she will yearn for a man to provide that protection. This, not sexual desire, is what the Torah means when we are told that God tells woman "your urge shall be for your husband" (*B'reishit* 3:16). When the Torah continues and God says, "He shall rule over you," this is not prescriptive. It rather describes woman's Faustian bargain for safety.[12] Man, in turn, is told that he will have to struggle against an unforgiving soil yielding thorns and thistles to eke out survival for himself and his family until he returns inevitably to that soil in death.

This is grim by any interpretation. But the story does not end on that note. To return to the point already made in the second

10. מ. ד. קאסוטו מאדם ועד נח (Magnes Press, 1959), 72–74.

11. See דעת מקרא בראשית א' (Mossad HaRav Kook, 1997), 80–81.

12. Ibid., 83. תשוקתך = מזונתך ופרנסתך ולפיכך "והוא ימשול בך". See also Rav Sa'adia ad locum.

essay, it is here that the Torah chooses to return to man's assigned role to name and classify the creatures God has made. Adam now turns to his wife and names her Hava (Eve), which as noted above is a name appropriate for her, because for Adam it means "the mother of all life" (*B'reishit* 3:20).

Chapter 4

Brotherhood and Murder

PARASHAT B'REISHIT

RAMBAN OBSERVES THAT ONE OVERARCHING THEME in the Torah narratives is the theme of exile as punishment for sin. Adam and Eve are exiled from the Garden of Eden and denied access to the tree of life. Cain kills his brother and he will be condemned to lifelong wandering upon the earth. With the great flood, antediluvian humanity will be completely driven off the earth. The aftermath of the Tower of Babel account will be the scattering of the nations (Ramban on *B'reishit* 1:1).

When Adam and Eve are expelled from the Garden, they are cast into a threatening, dangerous world. There is a well-known account in the Talmud that telescopes all of the events in the life of Adam and Eve from their creation until their expulsion from the Garden into the time frame of day six of Creation. Included in this time frame is the birth of Cain and Abel, the first two brothers, along with female counterparts (*Sanhedrin* 38b). Be that as it may, the Torah recounts the birth of the two brothers after the account of the expulsion from the Garden.

The Torah tells us that Adam "knew his wife," and their loving intimacy will produce children. When Eve was first separated from Adam's body, Adam exclaims that she will be called אשה – *isha,* woman, because she was separated from איש – *ish,* man. Adam assigns "his" woman the name חוה, "Eve."

When the first child ever born emerges from the body of the first mother, Eve, she exclaims, "I have fashioned an איש – *ish* together with God," and she now assigns her *ish*, or manchild, the name Cain (*B'reishit* 4:1). Thus both Adam acknowledges and names his wife, and his wife, in turn, acknowledges and names their child. This neat circle of generation seems initially utterly joyful.

But an ominous note is sounded when Cain's brother is born and named הבל, Abel, which means "breath" or "futility." This name anticipates his tragic, fruitless demise. Cain will murder his brother in a fit of jealous rage. Man's expulsion from the Garden constituted a rude awakening for him regarding his inescapable mortality. The first death will not be a natural event, but rather murder.

The two brothers grow up. Cain is a tiller of the soil while Abel is a shepherd, and both bring offerings to God from the fruits of their labor. But only with reference to the offering of Abel does the Torah say that Abel brings "the best of the firstlings of his flock." God then looks with special favor toward Abel's offering and Cain is overcome with jealous rage. God then turns to Cain and in poetic cadence says to him:

> לָמָּה חָרָה לָךְ וְלָמָּה נָפְלוּ פָנֶיךָ הֲלוֹא אִם תֵּיטִיב שְׂאֵת וְאִם לֹא תֵיטִיב לַפֶּתַח חַטָּאת רֹבֵץ וְאֵלֶיךָ תְּשׁוּקָתוֹ וְאַתָּה תִּמְשָׁל בּוֹ
> Why are you angry? Why is your face fallen? If you do well you will be uplifted. If you do not do well sin crouches at the door. Its urge is upon you but you can rule over it. (*B'reishit* 4:1–7)

There is a striking parallel in the language that describes Cain's ability to conquer sin and the language used by God in the curse imposed on Cain's mother after she and Adam eat the forbidden fruit of the tree of knowledge. There, God says to Eve:

> וְאֶל אִישֵׁךְ תְּשׁוּקָתֵךְ וְהוּא יִמְשָׁל בָּךְ
> Your urge will be for your husband and he shall rule over you. (*B'reishit* 3:16)

There God is speaking of woman's Faustian bargain with her

husband. She yearns for his protection and he in turn will rule over her. Here Cain is told:

> וְאֵלֶיךָ תְּשׁוּקָתוֹ וְאַתָּה תִּמְשָׁל בּוֹ
> [Sin's] urge will be upon you and you can rule over it. (*B'reishit* 4:7)

In effect, God is telling Cain that he can gain mastery over sin. Whatever the motivation, whatever the rage in your breast, you have the capability and the prerogative to choose to master your passions. You can suppress the temptation to sin.

But Cain does not exercise the prerogative of moral constraint. He surrenders to his rage and he murders his brother. God appears to Cain after the murder of Abel with a simple question: "Where is Abel, your brother?" Cain vainly attempts to shrug off the question: "I don't know! Am I my brother's keeper?" But there can be no escape from the truth in God's presence. God confronts Cain with his deed. "What have you done? Listen! Your brother's blood cries out to me from the earth" (*B'reishit* 4:8–10).

The Mishna in Tractate *Sanhedrin* notes that the Torah's term for blood here, *d'mei,* is given in the plural. It proceeds homiletically to make the point that not only Abel's blood, but the blood of all the children and children's children that might have issued from Abel, had he been allowed to live, cry to God from the earth. The murder of a single human being means the destruction of infinite possibilities. He who destroys one life destroys whole worlds (*B'reishit Rabba* 4:5; *Sanhedrin* 37a).

Cain is now condemned by his Creator, and a great curse will issue from the very soil that opened its mouth to swallow Abel's body. Having violently torn Abel's life from him, returning his body to the earth, Cain will find neither sustenance nor solace from the earth. Rather he will be condemned to ceaseless wandering.

Cain now acknowledges the magnitude of his offense. "My sin is too great to bear." Ramban explains Cain's words to mean, "My sin is beyond forgiveness" (Commentary on *B'reishit*

4:13). Cain can have no home and his shame will cause him to vainly seek to hide from God's presence. Unprotected by that presence, Cain exclaims that whoever has the opportunity, will kill him (*B'reishit* 4:14). But God will not allow that to happen. He provides Cain with the proverbial "Mark of Cain," which in the narrative is not designed to destroy him but to protect him. Cassuto understands the protective mark of Cain as the Torah's protest against revenge killings.[13]

God proclaims, "Therefore whoever kills Cain, שבעתיים יקם," which commentators such as Rav Sa'adia Gaon, Rashbam, and Ramban understand to mean "will be punished sevenfold" – i.e. many times over (*B'reishit* 4:14–16).

One should not imagine that the punishment of endless wandering is trivial. When Cain has a son, he builds his son a "city," or a permanent home and a social environment. What Cain has lost forever he seeks to give his child (4:17).

There is an alternative reading for *B'reishit* 4:15. Following Targum Onkeles and Ibn Ezra, among other commentators, God's pronouncement means "Let no one kill Cain. After seven generations, retribution will be delivered."

The Torah lists seven generations from Cain to the children of Lemakh and his two wives, Adah and Zillah (*B'reishit* 4:17–20). After Lemakh's children, we know nothing more about Cain's descendants. After that, the great flood erases all life except for Noah and his children. But Noah descends from the alternate line of Seth born to Adam and Eve after Abel's murder.

There are two very different lines of interpretations here. For Rav Sa'adia, Rashbam, Ramban, and others, Cain's punishment is lifelong exile and it ends with his death. For Targum Onkeles, Ibn Ezra, and others, Cain's sin will hover over his descendants unto the seventh generation. Critical to the diverse paths of interpretation is the meaning of the cryptic song of Lemakh that seems to intrude from nowhere upon the account of the descendants of Cain. Lemakh is the sixth generation from Cain and the seventh generation from Adam and Eve. The sons of Lemakh

13. מ. ד. קאסוטו מאדם ועד נח (Magnes Press, 1959), 123.

are presented to us as the progenitors of the great crafts of cattle herding, instrumental music, and metal work.

Lemakh now turns to his wives and says:

Adah and Tsila hear my voice,	עדה וצלה שמען קולי
Wives of Lemakh, attend to my words,	נשי למך האזנה אמרתי
I have killed a man for wounding me,	כי איש הרגתי לפצעי
A mere child for bruising me.	וילד לחברתי.
If Cain is avenged sevenfold,	כי שבעתיים יקם קין
Lemakh, seventy-seven fold. (4:23–24)	ולמך שבעים ושבעה.

To what killing is Lemakh referring? Predictably, creative speculations have emerged in an attempt to fill in the blanks.

Ramban, following Midrashic precedents, understands the statements about killing as a rhetorical interrogative. "Have I killed anyone? Certainly not!" In Ramban's rendering, Adah and Tsilah are concerned about the very skills Lemakh's children have been allowed to cultivate (Commnetary on *B'reishit* 4:23). Especially troubling is the craft of metalworking, which allows for the fashioning of weapons of war. But Lemakh protests that those who foster new skills cannot be blamed for their misuse. If others misuse those skills, they are responsible. If Cain, who actually committed murder, could be protected by God, how much more so Lemakh and his sons who killed no one.

For Ibn Ezra, who understands God's words to Cain to mean that punishment for the crime will come in the seventh generation, a very different meaning is intended in Lemakh's song. Adah and Tsilah were initially reluctant to have children who would constitute that seventh generation. But, says Ibn Ezra, there is an underlying ambiguity in God's statement about when Cain's punishment would come. Lemakh is insisting that God's statement to Cain – שבעתיים יקם, "After seven generations, retribution will be delivered" – refers to the seventh generation after Adam, not Cain. The fated recipient of the threatened punishment is none other than Lemakh himself. But in fact, Lemakh is alive and well. God in his mercy has set aside the judgment.

Ibn Ezra reads Lemakh's song not as an interrogative but as a declarative statement and with reference to the future. "[Even] if I kill a man for wounding me, a mere child for bruising me, God who delayed Cain's judgment for seven generations, will surely delay mine for seventy-seven generations." In Ibn Ezra's reading, God's condemnation of Cain is rendered innocuous in the course of time.

A very different reading is offered by Malbim. In Malbim's view, Lemakh is striking fear into the hearts of his wives. In effect, he is telling his wives, "Do not rebel against me! I have killed a man. I am prepared to do it again."[14] Or as Cassuto puts it, Lemakh is celebrating his amoral prowess, boasting to his wives that he has the proven capability of murdering whoever crosses him. Cassuto reads the wounding and bruising as Lemakh's deeds against his victim.

I have killed a man with mere wounding,
A young man with mere bruising.[15]

Lemakh's perverse reading of God's promise to Cain is now rendered in the following way: If Cain, who killed his brother could be avenged seven times, I will be avenged seventy-seven times through my own prowess. Now this Lemakh is the man whose children cultivated wonderful skills. Perhaps the Torah is making the point that material progress and moral progress are by no means connected. Great craft can coexist with moral barbarism.[16]

In the Torah's account, Lemakh's children are the last of Cain's descendants before the great flood. The Torah will tell us that the flood is punishment for man's moral degeneration in which "the world is filled with injustice" (6:13). In Malbim's and Cassuto's rendering, the song of Lemakh sets the stage for the ominous Divine judgments against a brutal, immoral humanity. It is emblematic of the tragic turn in God's Creation.

14. Cited in Nechama Leibowitz, *B'reishit: New Translation,* Vol. I (Hemed Press), 56.
15. מ. ד. קאסוטו מאדם ועד נח, 163–164.
16. Ibid.

Chapter 5

Corruption, Erasure, and Renewal

PARASHAT NOACH

AT THE BEGINNING OF *PARASHAT NOACH*, we are told that the "earth became corrupt before God; the earth was filled with חמס – *hamas*." *Hamas* is usually, though not exclusively, identified with robbery and violent seizure in rabbinic literature. The scholar Moshe David Cassuto understands this term in the flood narrative to mean injustice.[17] This is adopted by the JPS translation of the Torah. In the *Da'at Mikrah* commentary of Yehuda Kiel, *hamas* is taken to mean murder and mayhem.[18]

In fact, the one crime that the Torah has already described is murder – the murder of Abel by Cain. The case of homicide is again cited and possibly celebrated in the song of Lemakh. When Noah leaves the ark, the Torah will explicitly legislate against murder. This commends the *Da'at Mikrah*'s identification of *hamas* with murder and mayhem.

Now the Torah reiterates that "all flesh corrupted its way on the earth" (*B'reishit* 6:12). The sages, in a well-known Midrashic tradition, understand this to mean that the animal species crossbred! The significance of this offense can only be understood against the backdrop of the description of Creation in the first chapter of *B'reishit* (See Rashi, Commentary on *B'reishit* 6:12).

17. מ. ד. קאסוטו, מאדם ועד נח (Jerusalem: Magnes Press, 1959), 35–36.

18. דעת מקרא בראשית א' (Jerusalem: Mossad HaRav Kook, 1997), 170. עיקר משמעותו של חמס במקרא הוא מעשה של שפיכת דמים

There the Torah describes the process of Creation as a series of progressive differentiations. When plant and animal life are created, the Torah tells us, nine times in all, that each life form was created למינו, למיניהו, למיניהם – "according to its species." The Halakha then prohibits the crossbreeding of animals and the crossgrafting of plants (*Vayikra* 19:19, *Sifra Kedoshim* 4:13–17). This prohibition is considered universally binding (Tractate *Kiddushin* 39a, Rashi ad locum).

Whether or not this Midrashic tradition is the literal intent of the Torah's assertion that "all flesh corrupted its ways," it focuses our attention on something undoubtedly intended in the text, namely the blurring of the boundaries of God's creative work, which confers integrity upon its separate parts – its species.

When the great flood comes, the Torah tells us:

> נִבְקְעוּ כָּל מַעְיְנֹת תְּהוֹם רַבָּה וַאֲרֻבֹּת הַשָּׁמַיִם נִפְתָּחוּ
> The wellsprings of the great primordial sea (*t'hom rabba*) burst open, and the windows of the heavens were unsealed. (*B'reishit* 7:11)

When man erases the moral boundaries, which were his charge, then the punishment is delivered measure for measure. God erases the very boundaries that give solidity to man's world. The lower waters of the primordial sea suppressed by the dry land created on day three of Creation, and the upper waters of the heaven suspended above on day two of Creation, burst through their respective boundaries, returning the earth perilously close to the watery abyss out of which it was created in the first place. In effect, God's artwork is erased almost to the beginning.

Noah alone in his generation is found upright and wholehearted as he walks in God's presence. Together with his wife, his three sons and their wives, and along with representative pairs of each species, Noah survives in the ark. In effect, the ark is an incubator for an unsullied sampling of man and beast saved to renew the earth.

In preparation for the flood, Noah is given two separate commands to garner the representative pairs of animal species to survive and renew the earth. Two distinct names for God are used in the Torah's account of these two commands respectively.

Firstly, Noah is commanded to take two of each species of animal life into the ark. Here the name that is used for God is E-lohim (*B'reishit* 6:13–21). But then, when it is time for Noah to actually enter the ark, he is addressed by God using the Tetragrammaton, the Divine name Y-H-V-H, which we pronounce A-donai. He is now told to take seven pairs each of all the "pure" animals into the ark. As will be made clear, these seven pairs will be needed for Noah to offer sacrifices to God when the flood ends and Noah can leave the ark. Sacrifices are frequently offered in sevens (*B'reishit* 7:1–2; 8:20–22). Presumably, the "pure" animals are those animals the Torah will later permit to Israel for consumption. These are the animals that will be appropriate for Noah's offering.

The dominant theory of modern critical Bible scholars that assigns these two names and their commands to different documentary sources of the Torah is well known. But the sages understood the significance of these two names differently. E-lohim is broadly understood to denote God's strict justice whereas the Tetragrammaton usually represents the quality of Divine mercy or compassion. To put it differently, E-lohim suggests God's remoteness, whereas the Tetragrammaton denotes God's personal interaction with man.

In the first chapter of *B'reishit,* the Tetragrammaton is not used anywhere. There, Creation is presented in grand and ultimately impersonal terms, and for this, E-lohim is the appropriate designation. In the second Creation account of chapter two, the Tetragrammaton is used together with E-lohim. In the terms of the sages, שם מלא על עולם מלא – "The whole name over a whole world." There man is addressed in personal terms by a personal God.

When Noah is commanded to construct the ark to incubate the elements of renewed Creation while the flood rages on the earth, the name E-lohim is used alone just as it is used in chapter one of *B'reishit*. In the ark, a new world is being prepared while the old world is being destroyed. But when Noah's personal relationship with God is being singled out in the preparations for his offerings before God, the Tetragrammaton, God's personal name, is evoked in the text.

When the floodwaters recede and the land dries, God reveals himself as E-lohim and permits Noah and the other denizens of the ark to enter upon the new earth (*B'reishit* 8:15). When Noah builds an altar and offers his sacrifices, he does so to Y-H-V-H (*B'reishit* 8:20–21).

A new world requires a new dispensation. God then blesses Noah with fruitfulness as he blessed Adam with fruitfulness. When Adam was created, he was given dominion over all creatures but was only permitted to eat the vegetation of the earth (*B'reishit* 1:29–30). But Noah is permitted to eat the flesh of every creature and he is told that in his presence, fear and trembling will grip the other species. One restriction will apply. The flesh and possibly the blood of creatures still alive remain forbidden (*B'reishit* 9:2–4). It is as if a concession is now being made to man's bloodlust and this is to be satisfied in the dispensation to eat meat. As God states the matter, "the yearnings of the human heart are evil from man's first stirrings" (*B'reishit* 8:21). But even in this less exalted, postdiluvian world, murder will not be tolerated. "He who sheds the blood of a man, by man will his blood be shed, for in God's image did God make man" (*B'reishit* 9:6).

In Jewish tradition, we commonly speak of "the seven commandments of the children of Noah" as the fundamental religious, moral, and legal code binding all of humanity (Tosefta *Avoda Zara* 9:4, *Sanhedrin* 56a–59a). In the Talmud the issue of the Noahide code is complex. Rabbi Yohanan attaches the standard list of these commandments to *B'reishit* 2:16, where Adam is explicitly forbidden to eat the fruit of the tree of knowledge. If so, the list predates Noah and the flood. Indeed, different sages held different views about these rules and their origin. But the Torah text clearly prohibits murder here. It permits the consumption of meat, and prohibits consumption of the flesh of a living animal.

After the flood, God enters a covenant with Noah. A covenant is a binding agreement and in this covenant, God promises to never again bring the kind of flood that destroys the regularities of the earth and its seasons (*B'reishit* 8:22, 9:11). In the covenant passage, the word for covenant, ברית, appears seven times. Seven is the number that symbolizes wholeness in the Torah (*B'reishit* 9:8–17).

The sign of this covenant is the rainbow. In the Torah's words:

> אֶת קַשְׁתִּי נָתַתִּי בֶּעָנָן וְהָיְתָה לְאוֹת בְּרִית בֵּינִי וּבֵין הָאָרֶץ
> I have set my bow in the cloud as a sign of the covenant between me and between the earth. (*B'reishit* 9:13)

It is striking that the rainbow is said to appear in a cloud and this is repeated three times. We are told that whenever the rainbow will appear, God will "remember" his covenant between himself "and between every living being, all flesh that is upon the earth."

Now rainbows do not always appear in clouds. Cassuto assumes that this merely reflects a stereotypical phrase used in ancient literature.[19] In a different context, in the chariot vision of Ezekiel, we have an analogous usage. There the prophet describes his epiphany with the words:

> כְּמַרְאֵה הַקֶּשֶׁת אֲשֶׁר יִהְיֶה בֶעָנָן בְּיוֹם הַגֶּשֶׁם כֵּן מַרְאֵה הַנֹּגַהּ סָבִיב הוּא מַרְאֵה דְּמוּת כְּבוֹד ה'
> Like the appearance of *the rainbow, which is in the cloud* on a rainy day; such was the appearance of the image of light around; this was the appearance of the image of the Glory of God. (Ezekiel 1:28)

Perhaps the cloud is always cited in connection with the rainbow to contrast the revelation of God's covenantal sign with the darkness of the threat of destruction, as is suggested by Rashi in his commentary on 9:14.

As Rav Sa'adia Gaon, Radak, and Ramban, among others, remark, the rainbow is a natural phenomenon, the prism effect of light passing through the moisture in the atmosphere. But even natural occurrences can take on special meaning in the context of human experience. These special meanings can be multifaceted. In the context of the flood narrative and its aftermath with the rainbow, God "remembers" and will spare his creatures

19. מ. ד. קאסוטו, מאדם ועד נח, 94–95.

total destruction, a testimony to God's providence extended to humanity.

The rainbow has the appearance of a warrior's bow with its string placed upon the earth as a sign of peace. No arrows can be shot as long as the string lies immobilized upon the ground. No divine arrows are being aimed at those on earth. The multiple colors of the rainbow suggest modulation and nuance in God's judgment of human failings. In the terms employed by Ramban, the transformation of colors reflects a softening of Divine justice – מדת הדין רפה (Commentary on *B'reishit* 9:14).

Finally, the rainbow takes the form of a line across the sky. God created his world by drawing lines through the primal chaos. Morality is attained when human beings draw lines against their own instincts and impose boundaries upon human behavior. Even God, so to speak, draws lines in rendering judgment upon the earth. The rainbow, a phenomenon in the natural order, becomes a symbol of Divine self-limitation and a model for human constraint. It is placed against a backdrop of the dark cloud of destruction, extending hope in the postdiluvian order.

Chapter 6

God, Man, and Monuments: The Tower of Babel

PARASHAT NOACH

After the flood, Noah becomes the second Adam: father of postdiluvian humanity. Seventy nations emerge from Noah's children and are carefully classified and listed. The Torah concludes this account with the words, "these are the families of the children of Noah according to their origins and their nations; from them were the nations divided upon the earth after the flood" (*B'reishit* 10:32).

This new humanity, we are told, "had one language and the same words," and together they settled in the Shinar valley (*B'reishit* 11:1). A plan is advanced to build a great city with a tower whose summit reaches the sky. The builders say, "we will make a name for ourselves" and the human community will remain united and not be dispersed over the surface of the earth (*B'reishit* 11:1–4). But God nullifies this plan by confounding human language so that each subgroup spoke its own language incomprehensible to the next. The population, now divided by language, was spread upon the earth, and the great building project came to naught (*B'reishit* 11:5–8).

The Midrash comments, "The sins of the age of the flood are clearly explained, but the sins of the age of dispersion (Tower of Babel) are not clearly explained" (*B'reishit Rabba* 38:6). Indeed, the story is cryptically presented in a mere nine verses (*B'reishit* 11:1–9). Not surprisingly, different explanations emerged.

Rashbam asks in straightforward fashion "What was the sin in all of this?" Together with other commentators (Ibn Ezra,

Radak), who Ramban dismissively calls "the pursuers of plain meaning," Rashbam maintains that it was simply that God had a different plan for mankind. The Divine plan was for the earth to be populated broadly, and for this reason the human plan was nullified (Rashbam, Commentary on verse 4; Ramban, Commentary on verse 2).

But other commentators, including Ramban, find more sinister motives in the city and tower project. In the Talmud and related sources, stress is placed upon the ambition to build a tower that reaches the sky. The implication drawn here is that this united human community had decided to storm the heavens in order to wage war against God. The Talmudic Aggada identifies three groups among the builders. One group sought to enthrone man in place of God. A second group sought to erect an idol in the heavens. A third group was simply invested in an anti-God war. In this ambition to build the city and tower of man, the sages identify metaphysical rebellion (*Sanhedrin* 109a). Building upon this general approach, Ramban understands the sin as polytheistic heresy.

In the late Midrash, *Pirkei de R' Eliezer*, the few verses of the Torah's account is expanded into a fuller narrative. This generation constitutes a pagan kingdom ruled by Nimrod who appears earlier in the Torah as a man of power, "a mighty hunter before God" who reigned "in Babel in the Land of Shinar" (*B'reishit* 10:8–10). Midrashic tradition does not view the designation of "mighty hunter before God" as complimentary. Nimrod is understood to be a brutal predator and a violent rebel against God's sovereignty. In *Pirkei de R' Eliezer*'s rendering, Nimrod is the leader of the great rebellion against God (Midrash *Pirkei de R' Eliezer* 24).

Don Yitschak Abarbanel dissents from this reconstruction of the Torah's account. Abarbanel locates the sin of the tower elsewhere; he connects it to the sin of man in the Garden of Eden.

Like Rambam in the *Moreh Nevukhim* (I 2), Abarbanel understands the primal sin of Adam to be a turning away from the tree of life, which symbolizes the adhesion to truth, and pursuing of the tree of knowledge of good and bad, which represents the ephemeral. But Abarbanel puts a unique twist on what the ephemeral means. For Abarbanel this includes all of the arts, technologies, and ambitions embodied in developed material culture. What humanity should have done from the beginning was to have cultivated a life close to nature without any need for advanced technologies and acquired luxuries. To put the matter bluntly, in his general views, though certainly not in the way he lived, Abarbanel was a medieval version of a hippie. The sin of Babel's builders lay in the abandonment of a life close to nature and the pursuit of an urban culture. The patriarchs of Israel were shepherds. Moses and David were shepherds. Shepherds approach the naturalist ideal. Building a city was sin enough to warrant dispersion. Material culture, with its attendant greed, violence, and pursuit of power, was the evil that God sought to nullify.

Material culture and the pursuit of diverse technologies produce the need for new and complex languages, and it is this that divides humanity. And this same lust for material culture characterizes the primal error of Adam and Eve in the Garden of Eden (Commentary on *B'reishit* 11:1).[20]

Abarbanel's views, although intriguing, are extreme and not especially convincing as commentary on the Torah's narrative. However, there is one aspect to his interpretation that warrants careful consideration: namely Abarbanel's insistence on a parallel between the Tower story and the story of the Garden of Eden. But first we must consider some historical facts.

Thanks to modern archaeology, we now know that there was a literal Tower of Babel located in the city of Babylon. This kind of tower was known as a ziggurat, and it served as a pagan shrine. It was a multistoried building and it served as a central landmark in Mesopotamian cities. The ziggurat in Babylon, devoted to the god Marduk, was known as the "place of the foundation of heaven and earth." It was a source of pride and self-congratulations for its powerful builders.[21]

But from the perspective of the Torah, this Tower of Babel

20. אברבנאל על התורה כרך א' (Hotsaot Seforim B'nei Arbel, 1964), 171–181.

21. *The J.P.S. Commentary: Genesis* (Jewish Publication Society, 1989), 80–81. See also Cassuto מנח עד אברהם, (Magnes Press, 1959), 155–158.

embodied human vanity and arrogance, the deification by man of the works of his hands. As the commentators insist, there is no reason to believe that the builders literally thought that their tower would reach the sky. Rather they were building what we might call a "skyscraper" that would serve as a monument to their skill and power. Furthermore, this city and its tower would serve to concentrate the human race in one place under a single authority and would be a permanent monument to the builders.

Let us re-examine the narrative in the light of the above. In verse four, word goes forth:

> ויאמרו הבה נבנה לנו עיר ומגדל וראשו בשמים ונעשה־לנו שם פן־נפוץ על־פני כל־הארץ.
>
> Let us build ourselves a city and a tower whose pinnacle *reaches the sky, we will make a name for ourselves* lest we be scattered over the earth. (*B'reishit* 11:4)

Then the Torah presents God's reaction.

> וירד ד' לראת את העיר ואת־המגדל אשר בנו בני האדם.
>
> God *descends* to see the city and tower that humanity has built. (*B'reishit* 11:5)

From the perspective of the builders, they are reaching to the sky with their monumental edifice. But from God's perspective, it is such a puny affair that He must descend to see it. He then says,

> הן עם אחד ושפה אחת לכלם וזה החלם לעשות ועתה לא־יבצר מהם כל אשר יזמו לעשות.
>
> They are one people with one language for all of them. Having begun here, now nothing will be held back from them; whatever they decide to do they will do! (*B'reishit* 11:6)

God is mocking them with feigned shock and wonder at human prowess. He is mocking their unhinged delusion of grandeur. Herein lies the connection to the Garden story.

In the Garden narrative, the snake succeeds in tempting woman to sin by convincing her that eating from the tree of knowledge will make her and her husband godlike with their newfound knowledge of good and bad. The real consequence of violating God's command will be expulsion from the Garden and all of the other consequences of that expulsion. God then says to his angels:

> הן האדם היה כאחד ממנו לדעת טוב ורע ועתה פן־ישלח ידו ולקח גם מעץ החיים ואכל וחי לעלם.
> Man has now become like one of us knowing good and bad; now what if he reaches and takes from the tree of life and lives forever! (*B'reishit* 3:22)

But of course God will allow no such thing. Man is not godlike after all. God is merely mocking man's vanity; now man's fate is sealed. So too, in the Tower story man's vanity is mocked and nullified. God says to his angels:

> הבה נרדה ונבלה שם שפתם אשר לא ישמעו איש שפת רעהו.
> Let us therefore descend and confound their language so that no one will understand the language of his fellow. (*B'reishit* 11:7)

In the words of the Psalmist, "He who sits in heaven laughs" at human vanity and arrogance (Psalms 2:4). Abarbanel's insistence on the connection between the Tower story and the Garden story is very much on target.

The Tower story hinges upon the issue of human language. It is as a single linguistic community that man engages in the work of the great building project. When this unitary linguistic community is broken apart by mutual incomprehension, the project must be abandoned.

Netsiv, in his *Ha'amek Davar* commentary, comments on the manner in which this narrative is introduced. Man possesses שָׂפָה אֶחָת וּדְבָרִים אֲחָדִים (*B'reishit* 11:1). In Netsiv's rendering, mankind shared a "single language and *few words*." Netsiv contends that God responds negatively not to the contents of those words, but rather to their paucity.[22] This reveals a narrowness of perspective, a poverty of the human spirit. Arrogance does not coexist with greatness. It is, in reality, limiting, and this limitation is by no means morally neutral. In *Pirkei de R' Eliezer*'s rendering of the story, we are told that as the building project proceeded, there was a shortage of bricks. When a brick fell to the ground and smashed, the builders would weep. But when a human being would fall to his death it was of no account.

When God confounds the linguistic unity of mankind, the city is abandoned and the people dispersed. The Torah editorializes on the entire affair:

> עַל כֵּן קָרָא שְׁמָהּ בָּבֶל כִּי שָׁם בָּלַל ה' שְׂפַת כָּל הָאָרֶץ וּמִשָּׁם הֱפִיצָם ה' עַל פְּנֵי כָּל הָאָרֶץ
> That is why its name is Babel, for God '*balal*' – confounded – the language of the whole earth and from there did he disperse them over the surface of the earth. (*B'reishit* 11:9)

The name Bab-El literally means something else. It means "the Gate of God." That conjures up all of the pretension and vanity of the building project. But the Torah now provides a playful and ironic exegesis of the name. The city and tower, far from being the Gate of God, is emblematic of something else – confusion and incomprehension. In the Talmud, arrogance is equated with idolatry (*Sotah* 4b). The arrogant man has deified himself. Perhaps this is what lies embedded in the Aggada mentioned earlier that portrays the tower builders as waging war against God.

One should not imagine that mere declarative monotheism protects us from emulating the sin of the tower builders. In the Talmud Yerushalmi (*Shekalim* 5:4) we are told that when one sage boasted that he had erected beautiful gates on the local house of study, Rabbi Mano responded with a verse from Hosea. "Israel has forgotten her Maker and has built palatial Temples" (Hosea 8:14).

But how shall we respond to the punishment of the division

22. העמק דבר על ספר בראשית, רב נפתלי צבי יהודה ברלין (Hotsa'at Avraham Yitshak Friedman), 75. דיבור המתחיל "ודברים אחדים".

of the human family and their loss of ready capacity to converse with each other?

Seforno insists that left to its own devices, humanity would have unreflectively assented to an idolatrous regime. A suffocating conformity would have settled upon mankind. In Seforno's words, "no one would ever seek to know his Creator and to comprehend that God fashioned everything" (Commentary on 9:6).

The new diversity now imposed upon man would finally prove enriching, and in that enriching diversity man would find God. The dispersion of the nations is what sets the stage for a great human advance: the mission of Abraham our father.

Chapter 7

Abraham: Odyssey and Exile

PARASHAT LEKH LEKHA

THE MISHNA IN *AVOT* notes that in the Torah's genealogy there are ten generations from Adam to Noah and ten generations from Noah to Abraham (5:2). This is certainly not accidental. Implied in this reckoning is the following: Just as Adam is the father of the human race, so too is Noah. No second flood will come to erase Noah's descendants in the way Adam's descendants were erased, necessitating a new beginning for man. Nonetheless, Abraham's emergence will mark a new turn in human affairs, a new beginning of the spirit. God will call to Abraham, sending him to a new land in order to be the father of a new people.

Abraham is told, among other things, וְנִבְרְכוּ בְךָ כֹּל מִשְׁפְּחֹת הָאֲדָמָה – "All the families of the earth will be blessed in you" (*B'reishit* 12:3). Here, the word וְנִבְרְכוּ – *venivrikhu*, is translated as "blessed." However, Rashbam understands this term to mean that "all the families of the earth will be grafted onto you" (Commentary on 12:3). Similarly, Rabbi Yehuda HaLevi in his *Kuzari* (4:23), says that at the time of ultimate Messianic redemption, there will be a "grafting" of the nations onto the central family tree of Israel, making the prophetic endowment of Israel a universal endowment. Whether Rashbam's rendering of *venivrikhu* is the literal meaning of this term in the Torah's text or not, clearly the Torah understands Abraham's mission to be of significance to the entire human race.

Once Abraham enters the land and begins to travel through

it from north to south, there is a famine. Abraham continues his southward journey out of the land and toward Egypt. As Abraham approaches Egypt, he turns to Sarah, his wife, and says to her:

> הנה נא ידעתי כי אשה יפת־מראה את. והיה כי־יראו אתך המצרים ואמרו אשתו זאת והרגו אתי ואתך יחיו. אמרי־נא אחתי את למען ייטב־לי בעבורך וחיתה נפשי בגללך.
>
> Now I know that you are a beautiful woman. When the Egyptians see you and say 'She is his wife,' they will kill me and let you live. Please say you are my sister that it be well with me and for your sake, they will let me live. (*B'reishit* 12:11–13)

An implication drawn by Rashi in Abraham's words is especially troubling. As Rashi understands these words, Abraham is, in effect, saying, "We can turn this dangerous situation to profit. If you say you are my sister, it will be well with me because of you and they will present me with gifts" (Commentary on *B'reishit* 12:13). What kind of man uses the allure of his wife to tempt lascivious men in order to receive gifts? Indeed, why did Abraham go to Egypt in the first place? Now Rashi's comments are extreme, of course. Abraham may have simply meant that it "will go well with me and I will survive the danger through the stratagem of posing as your brother." But is this stratagem justifiable?

Radak assumes and indeed insists that the clear and present danger of Egyptian murderous lasciviousness only became apparent when Abraham and Sarah approached Egypt (Commentary on *B'reishit* 12:11–13). Abraham might have been killed and his wife seized. Dissembling, pretending to be sister and brother, afforded the couple time to deal with these dangers. Even in the barbarism of this circumstance, Sarah would not be subject to instant and repeated attack as long as the Egyptians believed that her acquisition could be attained in a bargain struck with her brother. The pretense created a modicum of protection for both Abraham and Sarah. Further, Radak insists that relying upon miracles rather than dealing realistically with the threat is never an acceptable option. Who is to say that a miracle will happen?

But Ramban will have none of this. He says, "Understand that Abraham sinned greatly if unwittingly here, drawing his saintly wife into the path of grievous sin because of cowardice in the face of death. He should have trusted that God would save him and his wife . . . Furthermore, his abandonment of the land he is commanded to inherit because of famine was sinful." Ramban concludes that it is this behavior that will condemn Abraham's and Sarah's descendants to Egyptian slavery (Commentary on *B'reishit* 12:11–13).

Setting aside for the moment whether Radak or Ramban has the better handle on the force of the narrative, one aspect of Ramban's comments is undoubtedly correct. There is a striking parallel between the elements of Abraham's descent to Egypt and Israel's later descent there. Let us review the elements of Abraham's descent.

Abraham and Sarah descend because of famine in Canaan. Once there, they fear that Abraham will be killed and Sarah spared because of her beauty. In fact, Sarah is seized and taken to Pharaoh's bedchamber. God strikes Pharaoh and his household with plagues. Abraham is summoned to Pharaoh and rebuked for the deception, but both Abraham and Sarah are freed and sent away from Egypt laden with wealth. Following Midrashic tradition, Ramban points to the parallels in Israel's later story. Israel too, will descend to Egypt because of famine. A decree will be issued to kill the male children and to spare the females. In the end, Pharaoh and all Egypt are struck by plagues. Israel will be released and sent away from Egypt laden with wealth. Thus the life of the father will serve as a signpost for the future history of the children.

The dissembling of Abraham and Sarah posing as brother and sister will occur once more when the couple enters the realm of the Philistines. Once again, the king will seize Sarah and she will be saved miraculously. The king will rebuke Abraham for this deception, and Abraham will explain his actions with the following words:

> כי אמרתי רק אין־יראת אלקים במקום הזה והרגוני על־דבר אשתי. וגם־אמנה אחתי בת־אבי היא אך לא בת־אמי ותהי לי לאשה. ויהי כאשר התעו אתי אלוקים מבית אבי ואמר לה זה חסדך אשר תעשי עמדי אל כל־המקום אשר נבוא שמה אמרי־לי אחי הוא.
>
> I thought that that there would be no fear of God in this place. They will kill me because of my wife. In truth, she is my sister: my father's daughter although not my mother's daughter, who became my wife. When God took me wandering from my father's house, I said to her, "This is the kindness you can do for me; wherever we go, say about me 'He is my brother.'" (*B'reishit* 20:11–14)

Apparently, then, this dissembling was planned from the beginning of the couple's travels. Radak softens the dishonest implications by insisting that this plan was put in place where it was necessary to avert imminent danger (Commentary on *B'reishit* 20:13). The text testifies to the pretense only with regard to Egypt and Philistia.

But Ramban, always sensitive to moral implications in these narratives, rejects Abraham's rationalization according to which his words were always technically true. In Ramban's words, "Even if it were true that Sarah was both his sister and his wife . . . his intention was to mislead. In this he sinned against [the Philistines] leading them toward serious sin. There is no difference whether the matter is true or false" (Commentary on *B'reishit* 20:12).

It is in fact striking that when this king, Avimelekh, restores Sarah to her husband, he pays damages to the couple, but then remarks to Sarah, "I have given one thousand silver pieces to your *brother*" (*B'reishit* 20:16). It is difficult to see this remark as anything other than a sarcastic, biting statement laden with contempt. This would seem to lend force to Ramban's evaluation of Abraham's behavior.

We have already observed the parallel between Abraham's descent into Egypt and Israel's later descent there. We have noted the Midrashic interpretive principle so important to Ramban that events in the life of the fathers become a signpost in subsequent Israelite history. Reflecting on that notion as we consider the dissembling of Abraham and Sarah in both Egypt and Philistia, perhaps we can say that the Torah is noting a tragic flaw in the Israelite national character that makes Israel prone to defeat and exile. In Ramban's terms, those flaws would be cowardice, failure of nerve, and inadequate faith.

It must be quickly added that the Torah will provide for more heroic descriptions of Abraham as well. When Lot, Abraham's nephew, along with the inhabitants of the Jordan region, is carried off into captivity by the invading four kings led by Chedarlaomer, Abraham hastily convenes his men and overtakes the enemy, rescuing the captives. He is now celebrated as a hero and hailed by kings (*B'reishit* 14).

Let us examine the aftermath of this narrative. From the beginning of *Parashat Lekh L'kha*, Abraham was promised that he would be the progenitor of a great nation and would inherit the land. In fact, Abraham was childless and, at most, a resident alien in the land. After the defeat of the four kings and the rescue of the captives, God promises Abraham protection and great reward. But taking stock of his barren state, Abraham asks to what avail are God's promises as long as he is childless and only his steward, Damesek Eliezer, will inherit him? But God now assures him that descendants issuing from his own loins will be his heirs. The Torah now notes that Abraham trusts God's promise and that this pure trust will count as special merit (*B'reishit* 15:1–6).

A second revelation follows the first in its train. God once again promises Abraham the inheritance of the land. But here Abraham asks, בַּמָּה אֵדַע כִּי אִירָשֶׁנָּה – "How shall I know that I shall possess it?" (*B'reishit* 15:8).

This question seems odd coming just after Abraham accepts the promise of children on faith alone without asking for any special signs. One explanation found in the Talmud and Midrash (*Ta'anit* 27b, *Megilla* 31b, and *B'reishit Rabba* on these verses) construes Abraham's question to be: "By what merit will my descendants inherit the land?" This rabbinic tradition takes its cue from the specific acts that God now tells Abraham to perform. Abraham is now commanded to take calves, sheep, goats, a turtledove, and a young bird as items in an elaborate ceremony. Each of these kinds of animals will be used in the sacrificial rites that the Torah will subsequently mandate for the people of Israel. Following this rabbinic tradition, Abraham is being told that his descendants will merit inheriting the land through acts of atonement largely involved in the sacrificial rites.

Both Radak and Ramban note that there is a difference between the promise of children, for which Abraham needs no sign and accepts on faith, and the promise of the land. Abraham will begin to see the blessing of children while he yet lives. The inheritance of the land will only occur in the course of history after Abraham has died. Perhaps the promised descendants will persist in a state of unworthiness. Perhaps the aboriginal Canaanite inhabitants will undergo moral improvement sufficiently regenerative to spare them destruction. Abraham is asking what will guarantee his descendants' claim to the land given the variables inherent in any historical process. According to the abovementioned rabbinic tradition, everything will depend upon the implementation of the sacrificial rites. But this explanation presents many difficulties.

It is striking that no altar is used here, and an altar is critical to any sacrificial rite. In fact, in rabbinic tradition this enactment is known as the Covenant Between the Parts. Abraham is commanded to take these animals and to cut them into parts, but not to offer them upon an altar. Dividing the animals and laying out the parts is the mark of a covenantal ceremony, rather than sacrifices. By way of example, in the last days of the first Temple, Jeremiah, at God's command, enacts a covenant in Jerusalem according to which the owners of Hebrew slaves will obligate themselves to set them free. To formalize this covenantal commitment, a calf will be cut in half and the slave owners will walk between the parts (Jeremiah 34:8–22). The point of the ceremony would seem to be that just as only the union of the two halves of the animal enables it to live, so too, both parties to the covenant commit to living together through mutual adherence to their agreements.

Abraham is dividing the calves, goats, and sheep. God will make specific commitments about the inheritance of the land,

and a smoking furnace and a flaming torch will pass through the parts, thus signifying God's promise to Abraham. Far from being offered as a formal sacrifice, these parts are exposed to birds of prey, which swoop down on the parts, and Abraham will chase them away in order to protect the carcasses that serve to formalize the promise.

There are other specifics cited here of great importance to the meaning of this revelatory event. God commands Abraham to take three calves, goats, and sheep; a three year old calf, goat, and sheep; or perhaps, a calf, goat, and sheep third born to its mother. The language of the Torah is ambiguous and all three possibilities mentioned here are considered by various commentators. But what is not in doubt is that the number three is being stressed. These three animal types are each divided in half. However, the turtledove and young bird are not cut but are apparently allowed to fly away in freedom. After Abraham chases away the birds of prey, he falls into a deep sleep, which is accompanied by feelings of terror. Then God speaks and tells Abraham that his descendants will be strangers in a land not their own. They will be enslaved and oppressed for four hundred years. The oppressing nation will be punished by God, and in the end, the descendants will go free with great wealth. God then says: "The fourth generation will return" to inherit the Promised Land (*B'reishit* 15:9–20).

Apparently, the cut animal parts serve to symbolize the three generations of the enslaved. The fourth generation of freedom is symbolized by the uncut birds, which can fly free. This is the explanation found in the commentaries of Rabbi Samson Raphael Hirsch, Rabbi David Tsvi Hoffman, and Rabbi Benno Jacob.[23]

Let us now return to the promise of children. Ten years pass since Abraham and Sarah have entered the land, and they remain childless. At Sarah's insistence, Abraham takes Sarah's slave Hagar as a concubine. Hagar conceives, but her pregnancy strengthens her sense of independence and equality with her mistress. Sarah demands the right to retaliate and punish Hagar. The now persecuted slave runs away. An angel appears to her

23. Nechama Leibowitz, *New Studies in B'reishit*, 149–150.

at a well, and tells her to return and to be patient under Sarah's persecution. He tells her that she is destined to give birth to a child who will be a progenitor of a great nation in his own right. She is instructed to call this child Ishmael for God has heard, שמע – *shama,* her cry. Hagar is reassured and returns to her mistress (*B'reishit* 16:1–16). Ramban, again sensitive to moral issues in the text, insists that Sarah has sinned in this persecution and that this will produce dire consequences for Sarah's own descendants (Commentary on *B'reishit* 16:6).

Now it is striking that Hagar is identified as an Egyptian (*B'reishit* 16:3). Here, an Egyptian slave is being persecuted by Sarah. This account is presented immediately after the Covenant Between the Parts, in which Abraham learns that his descendants will be enslaved. It will be Hagar's people that will be the enslaving nation.[24] In this way, the narrative of the emerging chosen people of God is woven like a fabric of moral consequence that testifies to the Divine governance always at work. Both the moral strengths and the moral weaknesses of Abraham and Sarah will shape the unfolding destiny of Israel.

24. JPS Torah Commentary, Genesis 119.

Chapter 8

New Names, New Covenants, New Meanings

PARASHAT LEKH LEKHA

In the first chapter of *B'reishit*, one name alone suffices for the Creator: E-lohim. In the second chapter of *B'reishit*, in the continuing account of Creation, God is now called "Y-H-V-H E-lohim." As already noted in chapter five, the sages take E-lohim to represent the quality of strict justice and the Tetragrammaton to refer to the quality of God's compassion in His relationship to His creatures. In broader terms, E-lohim is distant and relatively impersonal. With Y-H-V-H, God becomes a personal God.

When Noah is set upon his mission, God initially addresses him with His name E-lohim (*B'reishit* 6:13). By contrast, when Abraham is first addressed by God and instructed to go to the Promised Land, he is addressed by Y-H-V-H (*B'reishit* 12:1). This cannot be accidental, and it defines Abraham's mission differently. At the outset, the relationship is personal. Y-H-V-H is Abraham's personal God, and Y-H-V-H is thus the God of Abraham, in a special sense.

When Abraham is victorious over the four kings led by Chedarlaomer, and when the captives are freed, Melkizedek, the king of Salem, greets him with bread and wine. The Torah tells us that this king was priest to E-l Elyon. Now El and Elyon were both names of gods in the Canaanite pantheon, However, the Torah tells us that Melkizedek served E-l Elyon, who was Creator of heaven and earth. He greets Abraham with the words:

ברוך אברם לא־ל עליון קנה שמים וארץ. וברוך א־ל עליון אשר־מגן צריך בידך.
Blessed be Abraham of E-l Elyon who has delivered your foes into your hand. (*B'reishit* 14:16–20)

When the king of Sodom, whose city was sacked by the four kings, offers Abraham the spoils of war, Abraham demurs with the words: "I raise up my hand to *Y-H-V-H, E-l Elyon*, Creator of heaven and earth that I will not even take a shoestring of yours . . ." (*B'reishit* 14:22).

By identifying Y-H-V-H with E-l Elyon, the Creator God of Melkizedek, Abraham drives home the distinct character of his own religious position without polemics or sermonizing of any kind. Abraham embraces Melkizedek's worship of the Creator and identifies the Creator with his own God. Thus he establishes the monotheistic character of that religious position, and in doing so, Abraham initiates a new way to speak about his God.

Immediately after the events involving Melkizedek, God promises Abraham great reward. Abraham, pondering his own childless state, responds to God's revelation and for the first time ever he calls God "A-donai Y-H-V-H" (*B'reishit* 15:2). The sages note this first-time, unique designation, by saying: "From the day that the Holy One, Blessed Be He, created the world, no one called Him Adon – Lord, until Abraham called him Lord" (*B'rachot* 7b).

In the context of this revelation and in the context of the Covenant Between the Parts that follows immediately in the text, Abraham introduces the name A-donai, again defining his relationship to God in a new way hitherto unarticulated.

As we all surely know, this new name A-donai is used by Jews as the liturgical substitute for the Tetragrammaton, which the Halakha restricts to the Temple in Jerusalem. Following his own understanding of a critical passage in the Talmud, Rambam denotes the name A-donai as the *Shem HaM'yuhad*, or the "designated name" of God, and he refers to the Tetragrammaton as the *Shem HaMeforash*, or the "wondrous name" of God (*Moreh Nevukhim* I 61).

According to Rambam, if someone imprecates the name of God using the name A-donai, this is as much a capital offense as employing the *Shem HaMeforash* in this act (*Yad HaHazaka, Hilkhot Avodah Zarah* 2:7).[25] While this ruling is not undisputed, it nonetheless invests profound sanctity in this never-before-used name introduced by Abraham. New names reflect an expanded religious consciousness.

Now we should not forget that not only God receives new names in our Parasha. The first patriarch and matriarch of Israel were initially known as Abram and Sarai. They too are given new, expanded names, Abraham and Sarah, in the context of a new revelation in which God also adds a hitherto unknown name to Himself. This takes place in the revelation of the Covenant of Circumcision.

In the revelation initiating the Covenant of Circumcision, God says to Abraham, "I am E-l Sha-dai" (*B'reishit* 17:2). This new name is of uncertain etymology and its meaning have been explained in a variety of ways.[26] Historically, this name has been translated as "Almighty." This apparently follows an ancient Midrash that treats this term as a combination of the prefix "she" and the adverb "dai" meaning "who is sufficient" or "who has sufficiency" (*B'reishit Rabba* 46:3). Indeed, Rambam follows this Midrash and takes this name to mean that God is sufficient within His own being or is absolute (*Moreh Nevukhim* I 63). Rashi follows the same Midrashic text in his commentary on *B'reishit* 17:2, and renders it to mean, "Who has sufficient divinity for every creature," making it one more statement of monotheism. Ibn Ezra, in his commentary on *Sh'mot* 6:3, cites Sh'muel HaNagid's explanation of the name, understanding its derivation from the Hebrew root שדד – *shadad*, which means to dominate or overwhelm. He takes this name to mean that God overpowers and transforms the power that allegedly comes from astral forces.

25. "There are those who say that one is subject to the death penalty only if the imprecation is directed at the name Y-H-V-H (and not A-donai), but I rule that with either name the violator is to be stoned." (Translation is author's own.) But see *Sanhedrin* 56a with Rashi's comments, ד"ה על שם המיוחד, which indicates that Rashi is among those authorities that dispute Rambam's ruling. See also *Keseph Mishna* to Rambam 2:7.

26. JPS Torah Commentary, Excursus II 384–385.

But let us consider the following. This name appears seven times altogether in the Torah, five times in *B'reishit*. In each instance in *B'reishit*, the name has some connection to procreation or progeny. In *Sh'mot* 6:3, we are told that God revealed himself to the patriarchs of Israel using this name. In his commentary on *Sh'mot* 6:3, Rashi contends that what the Torah is telling us is that the designation "E-l Sha-dai" speaks to God's promises of progeny to Israel's founding fathers. Whatever the etymology of this name, Rashi convincingly explains that it is connected to the Divine promise of progeny. This also explains why this is the name that introduces the Covenant of Circumcision. Circumcision is done in the organ of generation.

God begins by announcing that He is E-l Sha-dai and exhorts Abraham to walk in His Presence and to become whole. God then promises to vastly multiply Abraham's descendants. It is here that God first expands the name Abram to Abraham and the name Sarai to Sarah, and it is Abraham and Sarah who will found God's people together. This new covenant will be eternal. Abraham's descendants will inherit the land and God will be their God. This promise is to be made manifest with circumcision so that this sign of the covenant will mark every male in Israel both freeborn and slave. By marking the organ of generation, the male child's procreative capacity is consecrated to the covenant of God (*B'reishit* 17).

Centuries later, Malakhi, the last of Israel's prophets, addresses his remarks to returnees from the Babylonian exile in the period of *Shivat Zion*, or return to Zion during the latter part of the sixth and possibly the beginning of the fifth centuries BCE. He confronts those Jewish men who had presumably abandoned their Jewish wives left behind in Babylonia to marry non-Jewish women living in Judea. He tells them, "God is witness between you and the wives of your youth whom you have betrayed" (Malakhi 2:14). "Judah has defiled what is holy to God and what He loves, and has cohabitated with the daughter of an alien god" (ibid. 2:11).

As is well known, the children born to non-Jewish mothers are not Jews even if sired by Jewish fathers. In the period of *Shivat Zion* mentined above, Ezra and the authorities in Jerusalem eventually insisted that both the non-Jewish wives and their children be excluded from the community (Ezra 9–10). The covenant of circumcision, visible in the flesh of every Israelite male, testifies to the obligation to marry exclusively in the community and have children in that context. On the other hand, the womb of a daughter in Israel is a purifying mikveh for any child conceived by her (*Kiddushin* 77a). The male is obligated to father his children in that purifying mikveh and the sign of the covenant is the constant reminder. The mother alone transmits Jewish identity.

In Parashat Lekh Lekha, Abraham's mission initiates new relationships with God. These qualitatively new relationships are codified in new appellations for God. Abraham's meeting with Melkizedek elicits the name E-l Elyon. The special promises of progeny and homeland elicit the name A-donai. The Covenant of Circumcision is the occasion for the revelation of the name E-l Sha-dai. In that revelation, God expands the names of Israeli's progenitors into Abraham and Sarah.

In that final revelation of *Parashat Lekh Lekha*, Abraham is commanded to become whole even while he is commanded to circumcise himself. There is a paradox here. Abraham is to become whole by an act of self-mutilation in which the foreskin present in nature is removed. Rav Sa'adia Gaon contends that this removal of the foreskin is indeed part of what makes Abraham whole. Circumcision is the act of construction in the human body left to the human being himself in his capacity as partner with God in Creation (*Emunot VeDeot* 3:10). This seems to be confirmed in Halakha.

In Torah Law, circumcision is supposed to take place on the eighth day of a vaginally born healthy male even if that day falls on Shabbat. For all others, circumcision would constitute a violation of Shabbat law. The fundamental labor prohibitions on Shabbat are acts that are consciously constructive in nature, and in principle, destructive acts are not part of the repertoire of forbidden labors.[27] Why then, should circumcision, when not

27. *Hagiga* 10b, מלאכת מחשבת אסרה תורה – "The Torah forbids creative labor."

occurring on the eighth day of life, represent Shabbat desecration? It is seemingly a destructive act of mutilation?

In fact, the Halakha regards circumcision, when enacted as a covenantal act, to be intrinsically creative and were it not for the mandatory eighth day, it would be forbidden on Shabbat (*Shabbat* 106a). This would seem to confirm Rav Sa'adia's understanding of the meaning of the covenant of circumcision.

New religious possibilities are intrinsically creative. The human being created in God's image becomes God's partner in Creation with the discovery of these new possibilities. The world can then be refashioned for good, and this can be done by the human being.

Chapter 9

Isaac and the Ambiguity of Laughter

PARASHAT VAYERA

THE REVELATION OF THE COVENANT of Circumcision to Abraham contains within it an extraordinary personal promise. Sarah, Abraham's beloved wife, is to give birth to a child. This child will be the first *ben-berit*, or child of the Covenant of Circumcision, in whom all hope for the emergence of a covenanted people will be invested – a people whose very power of generation will be consecrated to the God of Abraham.

But in her youth, Sarah could not conceive. Now at the age of ninety, she is to conceive a child with Abraham, her one hundred year old husband! Is it any wonder that Abraham laughs when he hears the news? (*B'reishit* 17:17).

However, Targum Onkeles translates the word וַיִּצְחָק – *va-yitschak*, "and he laughs," using the Aramaic word וחדי – *vakhadi*, which connotes not the laughter of scorn and derision, but the laughter of celebratory joy.

It should be noted that in the Torah's rendering we are given Abraham's inner thoughts: "Shall a hundred-year-old man father a child? Shall a ninety-year-old woman give birth to a child?" Abraham further protests, "It is enough for me that Ishmael (Hagar's son) lives" (*B'reishit* 17:18). Clearly, Abraham is struck by the absurdity of the promise. But God insists that Sarah will indeed give birth, and that Abraham will canonize his own laughter in the child's name Yitschak, commonly transliterated as Isaac, which means laughter (*B'reishit* 17:17–19).

At some point after the Covenant of Circumcision is enacted by Abraham, three angels disguised as human beings visit him. They reiterate the Divine promise of a son to Abraham and in earshot of Sarah (*B'reishit* 18:1–11). Like her husband, Sarah too laughs and thinks to herself, "After I have withered, am I to have enjoyment with a husband so old?" (*B'reishit* 18:12).

But Onkeles translates Sarah's laughter differently than his translation of Abraham's laughter. Here he uses the Aramaic וחייכת – *vehayekhet*, which means that "she mocked."

God now reproves Abraham with the words, "Why has Sarah laughed? Is anything too wondrous for God?" Onkeles again translates Sarah's laughter as חייכת, that "she mocked." But in the Torah's text there is no difference at all in the terms used to describe both Abraham's and Sarah's laughter. Why then does Onkeles understand the two instances of laughter differently?

To understand Onkeles' distinction, one must only consider the differences between the sources of this remarkable news as heard by Abraham and Sarah respectively. Abraham hears the news in a Divine revelation. Abraham's understandable initial disbelief is due solely to the seeming absurdity of what is proposed. But this source does not lie, and after the initial shock, which induces laughter, there can only be joyful acceptance, which changes the meaning of that laughter into joy.

Sarah, by contrast, receives this information by overhearing the conversation of what appears to be human beings. Indeed, the Torah goes to great length to tell us that these beings participate in a feast in which they consume food like ordinary mortals. Receiving such information from human beings would lead any normal person to laugh in derision. This is what Onkeles seeks to capture in his artful and sensitive translation.

Now God censures Abraham for Sarah's mocking laughter, and when Sarah is confronted with the fact that she has mocked a Divine promise, her first instinct is to deny that she laughed at all (*B'reishit* 18:13–15). But she is told either by God or by one of the angels (the text is ambiguous), "No. You laughed!" All of this reinforces the requirement to name the promised wonder child Isaac.

Now the laughter surrounding the promise of this child does

not end with Isaac's conception. When Isaac is born, Sarah exclaims, "God has given me reason to laugh. Whoever hears will laugh with me" (*B'reishit* 21:6). Now the laughter here is unambiguously joyful and celebratory, and this is reflected in Onkeles' translations.

But a new problem now arises that will mar the joy. Abraham already has a firstborn son, Ishmael the son of Hagar! Sarah sees Ishmael and he is laughing (*B'reishit* 21:9). The *Midrash Rabba,* cited by Rashi, associates Ishmael's laughter with all manner of wickedness. But Onkeles, with great subtlety, translates Ishmael's laughter using the Aramaic term מחייך – *mehayekh,* "mocking."

Perhaps Ishmael was not really mocking, but merely laughing as children laugh. What the Torah tells us is that Sarah *sees him laughing*. Onkeles presumes that Sarah understands that laughter as mockery. After all, Ishmael was born first and by the normal rules should be Abraham's primary heir. In fact, the text strongly suggests that Sarah views Ishmael's laughter that way because what she now says to Abraham is, "Cast away that servant girl and her son, for that servant girl's son shall not inherit together with my son Isaac" (*B'reishit* 21:11). Great unease attaches itself to the child known as "laughter."

In the excruciating trial of the Akeda, God will test Abraham's faith by demanding that Abraham take that child whose name means laughter and offer him upon an altar. The child will be spared only after facing his own father's slaughtering knife. At that terrible moment who could have laughed except a heartless and spiteful scoffer?

As an adult, Isaac himself will be described once as laughing. This will happen in a tender moment that a husband is surely entitled to share with his wife. But the circumstances would not permit unalloyed joy. Isaac is a vulnerable alien in the Land of the Philistines. Like his father before him, Isaac had adopted the stratagem of pretending that Rebecca was not his wife but his sister. It was the king of the Philistines himself who caught a glimpse of a moment that gave away the game, revealing Isaac's true relationship with Rebecca. The king now forbids his subjects against predatory attacks upon Isaac and his wife on pain of death (*B'reishit* 26:8–11). But the safety and integrity of Isaac and Rebecca and their marital relationship depends upon the good graces of a sovereign of an alien people. There is no unalloyed joy and laughter where powerlessness reigns. Under such conditions, the ordinary joyful laughter of a husband and wife together is marred by their political powerlessness. In a striking passage, the Talmud says that "from the day the Temple was destroyed, the pleasure of sexual intercourse was taken away and given to sinners" (*Sanhedrin* 75a). When Isaac's descendants experience the catastrophe of defeat, destruction, and exile, all joy is muted and the normal pleasures of life can no longer be taken for granted. Powerlessness compromises laughter.

In the end, Isaac will become blind. In his blindness, he will be tricked by his son Jacob acting in league with his wife. This will be the fate of the patriarch whose name means laughter.

Abraham's name was transformed, and Jacob, the third patriarch, was given an entirely new name, Israel. Isaac's name always remains the same. But Isaac's name bears two meanings. One meaning is joy and the other is mockery. Of the two meanings, which one more accurately describes Isaac's life and legacy?

According to a well-known Midrashic statement favored by Ramban, the events of the lives of the fathers are a signpost for the children. What signpost are the people of Israel to read in the life of Isaac?

Chapter 10

Of Angels, Abraham, and Sodom

PARSHAT VAYERA

THREE ANGELS VISIT ABRAHAM to inform him of the imminent occurrence of Sarah's pregnancy with Isaac. But only two of these angels arrive in Sodom (*B'reishit* 19:1). The sages comment that each angel has but one task in this world. In the context of our narrative, one angel was sent to deliver the message of Sarah's pregnancy and with that task completed, that angel disappears. The two remaining angels have the respective tasks of rescuing Abraham's nephew, Lot, and destroying Sodom and her satellite towns (*B'reishit Rabba, Vayerah* 50:2). In this way, the sages are underscoring the seamlessness of the narrative that both herald the good news of Isaac's future birth and the cataclysm about to descend upon Sodom.

As soon as the angels depart from Abraham, the Torah presents God's thoughts. God says, "Shall I conceal what I am about to do from Abraham? Abraham is destined to form a great and numerous nation, through which all of the nations of the earth will be blessed. I have singled him out," ידעתיו – *yeda'ativ*, literally, "I have known him," "that he might instruct his children and household thereafter to keep God's ways doing what is just and decent" (*B'reishit* 18:15–19).

By contrast, there is an outcry concerning the extraordinary wickedness of Sodom and Gomorrah. "I shall descend and see whether what they have done is irredeemable, and if not, אדעה – I will know" (*B'reishit* 18:18–210). The same verb, ידע – *yada*, is used to describe God's singling out and "knowing" Abraham and his "knowing" the character of Sodom's wickedness.

When God says that he has "known" Abraham, Rashi avers that this knowledge is the knowledge that accompanies love. When God says that if there is mitigating circumstance in Sodom's wickedness "I will know," Ibn Ezra explains God's "knowing" here as implying "I will have mercy." God's knowledge of man is bound up with his concern for man.

Much later in the Torah, Israel will be commanded to love God unconditionally (*Devarim* 6:5). At the end of his *Sefer Mada* in the *Yad HaHazaka*, Rambam comments on this verse saying, "In equal measure to the knowledge will be the love" (*Hilkhot Teshuva* 10:6). In biblical usage, knowledge, love, and intimacy are all bound up together.

Here God tells Abraham that before judgment will be rendered against Sodom, God "will descend to see" the facts in Sodom. Rashi now delivers the exalted homily that this teaches the judges of future courts that visual proof must precede the pronouncement of a verdict of guilt in a capital case. But a deeper point is addressed by Ramban, who asserts that God knows individual human beings and extends His providence to them only if they are among His saintly ones. This is what the Torah means when it says that God has singled out and knows Abraham. In Ramban's words, "God's providence in the lower world guides the general (not the particular) and thus even individual human beings are governed by chance until it is time to judge them. But God grants His attention to His saints whom He knows as individuals with His guidance cleaving to them always" (Commentary on *B'reishit* 18:19).

Abraham alone is known by God, not the mass of humanity. But now Sodom is being singled out for judgment and this is expressed in God's "descent to see."

But this means that the case of Sodom is exceptional, and under general circumstances we cannot take God's providential intrusion into human affairs for granted. As the rabbinic aphorism has it, "The world follows its accustomed pattern," and God does not automatically guarantee either successful outcomes for the righteous or destruction for the wicked (*Avodah Zorah* 54:b).

But in this case, God announces His descent into human affairs to judge Sodom and Abraham is filled with trepidation. If the wicked city is condemned, what of the righteous minority in its midst? Abraham pleads their cause "for shall not the judge of all the earth do justice?" (*B'reishit* 18:25). Perhaps only fifty righteous people will be found in Sodom, or perhaps only ten. Will the minority of righteous be sufficient to save the city? But as we shall see, there are even less than ten in Sodom.

When the two angels arrive in Sodom, they find Abraham's nephew Lot at the city's gates (*B'reishit* 19:1). Earlier, when Abraham had returned from Egypt to Canaan, a bitter fight had engulfed the shepherds of Abraham and Lot. Abraham realized that he must separate from his nephew. He asked Lot to choose the location in the Promised Land in which he wants to settle, either to the north or to the south. But Lot chooses neither. He leaves the heartland of the Promised Land for the eastern periphery in the rich and verdant country of Sodom and Gomorrah, even though, as the Torah tells us, the inhabitants "were exceedingly wicked and sinful" (*B'reishit* 13:5–13).

But when the angels arrive in Sodom, Lot displays the same warm hospitality we have seen with regard to Abraham in greeting the visitors. However, the natives of Sodom are unreservedly hostile. They gather at Lot's house, where Lot has welcomed his guests, and demand that he surrender these strangers to the mob who say that they want to "know" them. Here knowledge means carnal knowledge.

If Lot is warmly welcoming to strangers, the natives of Sodom want only to visit sexual violence and humiliation upon them. Lot tries to protect his guests and, shockingly to our sensibilities, Lot, in desperation, offers to cast his virgin daughters to the mob in their stead (*B'reishit* 19:2–8). The sages express their own outrage at Lot's offer by commenting, "A normal man sacrifices his own life to save his daughters and his wife, fighting to the end, but this man is prepared to surrender his daughters to be raped!" (*Tanhuma Vayera* 15). Lot presents a mix of nobility and barbarism that respectively represents both the values of Abraham and Sodom.

Abraham was singled out by God's special providential guidance because God knew that he would teach his children the just and the decent. By contrast, Sodom is singled out for destruction because of its irredeemable lack of all decency. The narrative begins with Abraham's elaborate display of generosity to strangers who only retrospectively are revealed to be angels. That generosity of spirit is further revealed in Abraham's solicitous concern over Sodom's fate.

Sodom is destroyed because its response to the presence of strangers is the violence and humiliation described above. In Ezekiel 16:49, the prophet pinpoints Sodom's decisive sinfulness in its refusal to support the poor and needy though they were blessed with abundant wealth. The sages elaborate on this abominable selfishness, explaining that the Sodomites gloried in their wealth and were determined that no strangers should arrive to share their good fortune (Tosefta *Sotah* 3:3).

Generosity, as in the case of Abraham, brings God's providential solicitousness to human life. Selfishness destroys everything.

But now, let us consider the postscript in this narrative. What happens to Lot? The angels drag him and his immediate family from the city in the wake of Sodom's destruction. In the end, Lot finds himself alone with the two virgin daughters he was prepared to cast to the mob, in the mountains above the destroyed cities (*B'reishit* 19:29–30). The eldest of the two expresses her fear to her sister, "There will be no man who can be with us in the manner of the whole earth" (*B'reishit* 19:31). The sisters now conspire to render their father drunk on two consecutive nights and they each have relations with their father and become pregnant, allowing them a desperate future (*B'reishit* 19:32–38).

As the sages note, Lot was prepared to allow his daughters to be defiled by the Sodomite mob. In the end it is Lot, the father, who defiles them (*Tanhuma* 15). The motivations of both father and daughters come under discussion as well. But whatever the motivations, this constitutes a horrific climax to the horrific fate of the wicked city in which Lot chose to dwell.

Chapter 11

The Judgment of History and the Akeda as a Paradigm

PARSHAT VAYERA

WHEN RAMBAM, IN HIS *MOREH NEVUKHIM*, addresses the account of the Akeda, the binding of Isaac (*B'reishit* 22), one question especially vexes him. The Torah introduces this narrative telling us that God tested Abraham to determine his steadfastness or his reverence for God. Why would an omniscient God need a test to prove Abraham's faith and commitment?

When Abraham proves his faith by being prepared to sacrifice his son, an angel of God says, "Now I know that you revere God." Did God not know this from the beginning?

Rambam insists that the real point of the story of the Akeda is to serve as a paradigm for human commitment, that *we*, and not God, are made to know the lengths human beings must go in their obedience to God's command. In Rambam's words, this narrative serves "to teach us the boundaries of loving God, may He be exalted, and to what lengths revering Him must extend" (*Moreh Nevukhim* III 24).

He further elaborates:

> Abraham our father did not hasten to slaughter his son out of fear that God might kill or crush him, but solely because human beings are obligated to love and revere Him. It is not out of anticipation of reward nor fear of punishment.... Therefore the angel says to Abraham "Now I know that you revere God." This means that by this deed through which

you clearly revered God, all men will know how far reverence for God must go.

Now clearly there is a profound moral dilemma here, but let us set that issue aside for now. Let us first consider the nature of the paradigm.

Following Rambam's comments, Abarbanel seizes upon the Torah's use of the Hebrew word נסה – *nisa*, to express God's testing of Abraham. Abarbanel connects this verb with the Hebrew noun נס – *nes*, which means banner. Abarbanel now understands the first verse in the narrative to mean, "God raised Abraham aloft as an exalted banner."[28] This serves to underscore the idea that this narrative is designated to be paradigmatic.

Ramban avers that God's foreknowledge of Abraham's faithfulness would be insufficient as a model for us (Commentary on 22:1). That would only indicate the inclination of Abraham's heart. The test serves to render the potential actual by revealing Abraham's deeds. Only Abraham's actual deeds indicate his faith and shape his destiny.

In the Hellenistic period, during the tragic circumstances of forced apostasy at the hands of Antiochus IV, Jews who resisted those decrees and were prepared to pay the ultimate price, read the Akeda as a mandate for their sacrifice (*First Maccabees* 2, *Fourth Maccabees*). Forever after, the Akeda was taken as a paradigm for *Kiddush Hashem*, or ultimate sacrifice to sanctify God's name.[29]

In his commentary to the Torah, Ibn Ezra cites a jarring tradition that claimed that Abraham, in fact, slaughtered Isaac who was then resurrected. One senses this commentator's dismissive anger when he curtly states, "He who says this . . . turns Scripture upside down!" (Commentary on 22:19).

While it is hard to disagree with Ibn Ezra, it is more intriguing to ask what would have led to the emergence of such a seemingly perverse tradition.

28. פירוש על התורה דדון יצחק אברבנאל Vol. I (D'fus HaPoel, 1964), 267.

29. Cf. Shalom Spiegel, *The Last Trial: On The Legends and Lore of the Command to Abraham to Offer Isaac as a Sacrifice – the Akedah* (LongHill Partners, Inc., 2000).

In fact, if the Akeda is a paradigm for martyrdom, it proved to be too mild for the stark, tragic realities of Jewish history. Let us examine one version of the well-known tradition of "the woman and her seven sons" as it has come down to us in the Midrash *Eikha Rabba*.

In this rendering, each son, in sequence, refuses to accede to the will of Caesar and bow down to an idol at Caesar's command. One after the other each son expresses his defiance and is killed. When the seventh child is about to be killed, the mother pleads with Caesar, "By your life Caesar, give me my son so that I might hug him and kiss him." Caesar accedes to her request and the distraught woman bares her breasts to suckle him. She then pleads with the tyrant. "By your life Caesar, kill me first before you kill him." The tyrant refuses her plea, cynically using as his reason the Torah's dictum "You shall not slaughter a cow or sheep together with its young on the same day" (*Vayikra* 22:28). He issues the command for the child's immediate death. The poor mother falls upon her child hugging and kissing him and she instructs him, "My son, go to Abraham your father and tell him, 'This is what my mother has to say: Do not be arrogant and boast "I built an altar and offered Isaac my son upon it." [Tell him] "Our mother built seven altars and offered seven sons upon them on one day. For you it was a test. For me it was reality"'" (*Eikha Rabba* I:50).

In that powerful Midrash, it becomes all too clear that the Akeda narrative of the Torah had become a pale reflection of what Jews would endure countless times in their history. The odd revision of the Akeda cited disapprovingly by Ibn Ezra more closely approximated the horrors of centuries of *Kiddush Hashem* than did the actual passage of the Torah.

It was during the Crusades that the full horror of what some Ashkenazic Jewish communities felt impelled to do to resist apostasy, manifested itself.[30] In several communities, faced with the grim choice of apostasy or death, knowing full well that their surviving children would be forcibly baptized, these Jews slaughtered their children before killing themselves.

30. Cf. Shalom Spiegel, *The Last Trial*.

All this bears a striking resemblance to the mass suicide of the Jewish defenders of Masada in 73 CE recorded by Josephus (*Wars of the Jews* 7:8,9). There too, the Jews engaged in mass suicide rather than surrender to the Romans. But Josephus' writings were unknown to these Ashkenazic Jews and no Jewish tradition survived about the martyrs of Masada. It is remarkable that these medieval Ashkenazic Jews should have chosen a path already paved by the Jews of Masada, yet utterly unknown to them.

To quote a liturgical elegy we recite on the Ninth of Av in commemoration of these terrible events:

> Daughters of perfect beauty and babies just weaned from the breast were brought to slaughter like lambs and kids. A father subdued his compassion and consecrated his children to slaughter like sheep. The children said to their mothers, "We are to be slain," as the women designated the babes they so tenderly loved for killing, dragging them to the shambles.
>
> Who can hear this and not shed tears?
>
> The son is slaughtered and the father says *Shema*. Whoever saw anything like this? Whoever heard such a thing?
>
> The most beautiful portion of the household, the virgin daughter of Judea, stretched out her throat after sharpening her knife.
>
> God's eye saw this and bore witness.
>
> The distraught mother, her breath leaving her, completed all for slaughter as a rejoicing mother would prepare a meal.
>
> Young girls, both married and betrothed, danced joyfully to greet the killing sword and their blood poured out upon a dry rock left uncovered.
>
> The father turned, weeping and wailing, casting himself upon his sword, being pierced through, wallowing in blood, in the midst of the road. (*Kinot* for Tish'a B'Av, 31)[31]

31. For the most part, I have relied on the translation of Rabbi Abraham Rosenfeld in his superb presentation of the kinot in *The Authorized Kinot for the Ninth of Av*, 2nd ed. (London: C. Labworth and Company, 1970).

The fate of these martyrs became a dark but celebrated legend of what Rambam called "the boundaries of loving God, may He be exalted, and to what lengths revering Him must extend." This is the Akeda of early Ashkenazic Jewry, a commentary on the Torah written in the blood of unyielding, stubborn Jewish resistance to surrender.

What makes these awful events in the history of early medieval Jewry ever more remarkable is their apparent lack of strict Halakhic warrant. A Jew faced with the command to worship idols has a prima facia obligation to resist even with his life (Rambam, *Yad Hazak, Hilkhot Yesodei HaTorah* 5:1,2). But nowhere in normative Halakhic literature is that Jew authorized to take another's life to prevent future idol worship.[32] But here, religious instinct proved more powerful than canonized law. Jewish historical consciousness then canonized the deeds of the martyrs.

The frighteningly tragic history of Israel elevated the biblical narrative of the Akeda to a preeminent place among the many paradigms for Jewish commitment. It is in the context of Jewish historical consciousness that we must now turn to the actual story as it is written in the Torah.

32. In this context, see the comments of Rabbi Joseph Karo (author of the *Shulkhan Arukh*) in his *Beit Yoseph* to *Tur Yoreh Deah* 157 in his annotations marked as *Bedek HaBayit*. Translated here are just some of his comments taken from *Orhot Hayim*.: "In time of martyrdom it is permissible to sacrifice one's life even by one's own hands if he fears he will not be able to withstand the trials ... From this notion there were those who sought proof for their slaughter of children in times of apostasy. But many disagree ... It happened that one Rabbi slaughtered many children in the time of apostasy out of fear that they would be baptized. Another Rabbi was with him and in fury called him a murderer. But the first Rabbi ignored him. The second Rabbi said, 'If I am correct, let him die a horrible death.' And so it was." It is striking that while Rabbi Joseph Karo seems to agree with the second Rabbi, he adds no further personal comments.

Chapter 12

The Akeda: The Moral Paradox

PARSHAT VAYERA

THERE IS A WELL-KNOWN MIDRASH in which Abraham is confronted by the Satan or angelic adversary on the road to offer his son as a sacrifice on Mount Moriah. This angelic being turns to Abraham and exclaims, "Old man, old man, have you lost your mind? You were given a son at the age of 100 and now you are resolved to slaughter him?" Abraham responds, "Nonetheless!" Satan continues, "Tomorrow they will say to you, 'you are a murderer! You are guilty of murdering your son.'" Abraham again responds, "Nonetheless!"

Sensing that it was useless to try to dissuade Abraham, Satan now turns to Isaac, "You are a child of a suffering woman and he is going to slaughter you!" Isaac responds "Nonetheless!" (*B'reishit Rabba* 56:4).

Those who crafted this Midrash were clearly open-eyed to the horrific moral and personal dilemmas posed by this narrative. That it is Satan who raises the issues in no way vitiates their power.

When Abraham stood before God in advance of Sodom's destruction, he rhetorically asked, "Shall not the judge of all the earth do what is just?" The clear assumption underlying Abraham's dialogue with God is that God is indeed just. But here Abraham is commanded by God to do the morally unthinkable and Abraham does not flinch.

Abraham is commanded to take what he loves more than

anything else, "your son, uniquely yours, whom you love, Isaac," and offer him as a burnt offering (*B'reishit* 22:2). At the beginning of Abraham's odyssey, he was commanded to leave his land and family and go to a new land, yet to be revealed where he would become the father of a great nation in whom all of the families of the earth would be blessed. The term used to command him was לך לך – *lekh l'kha*, "go" (*B'reishit* 12:1). Now, using the same command of לך לך, Abraham is told to go to the Land of Moriah and offer his son and all of his hopes for the future upon one of the mountains yet to be revealed. It is as if all of Abraham's exertions in his obedience to God are now to be laid waste by yet one more command of God. God had promised Abraham, "Through Isaac will your seed be designated" (*B'reishit* 21:12). But now Isaac is to be slaughtered before there is any seed at all. All hope, including the hope for moral elevation, is now to be turned to dust.

On the third day of Abraham's journey to Moriah, Abraham spies the designated mountain from afar. He leaves behind his servants and donkey and proceeds alone with Isaac by foot, taking firewood, fire, and a slaughtering knife. The Torah records no initial explanation from father to son. It is Isaac who breaks the silence when he asks, "'I see the fire and the wood but where is the sacrificial lamb?' Abraham answers, 'God will designate the sacrificial lamb, my son.' And the two walk together" (*B'reishit* 22:4–8). Rashi captures the pathos of this brief exchange by paraphrasing Abraham's words, "God will designate the lamb, and if there is no lamb, the lamb will be you, my son."

The Midrash further comments on their walking together. "One goes to bind and the other to be bound [upon the altar], One to slaughter and the other to be slaughtered" (*B'reishit Rabba* 56:4).

Father and son arrive at the designated site but no further conversation is recorded. Abraham erects an altar, arranges the firewood, and ties down his son on top of the wood. He takes the knife in hand to slaughter his child. He is clearly prepared to do the deed. In the nick of time, an angel calls to Abraham from the heavens and tells him, "Do no violence to the child, nothing at all! Now I know that you revere God, not even withholding your son, uniquely yours, from Me." Abraham raises his eyes, spying a ram caught in the thicket by its horns. He takes the ram and offers it in place of his son (*B'reishit* 22:9–13). All of this is done without any comments from Abraham.

One must be struck by the cold silence of this entire narrative. Abraham only speaks in response to Isaac's brief query, and he is less than forthright. God has commanded and Abraham proceeds obediently and without argument. Whatever conflicting emotions there might have been in Abraham's heart, they nowhere figure in this narrative.

Much later, the Torah will reflect with horror on the pagan rites practiced by the aboriginal inhabitants of Canaan involving human sacrifice. It will forbid seeking out the rites of Canaanite worship for imitation. "You shall not do likewise for the Lord your God, for they did every abomination that God hates for their gods. They even burned up their sons and daughters in fire to their gods!" (*Devarim* 12:31).

When the Israelites of First Temple times in fact sought to imitate pagan rites and perform human sacrifices in the valley of Ben Hinom outside the walls of Jerusalem, the prophet Jeremiah expresses the horror of a follower of Moses' Torah when he denounces these paganized Jews in God's name. "They built shrines to *Ba'al*, burning their sons and daughters in fire to *Ba'al*, which I commanded not, of which I did not speak, and which did not enter My mind" (Jeremiah 19:5).

There is an especially striking comment made in a rabbinic homily on this verse in Tractate *Ta'anit*. "'Which I commanded not' – this refers to Mesha, king of Moab (who sacrificed his firstborn), 'Of which I did not speak' —this refers to Jefthah (who sacrificed his daughter in fulfillment of a vow), 'Which did not enter my mind' – *this refers to Isaac son of Abraham*'" (4a).

This sounds remarkably like a criticism of the account of the Akeda itself! In his comments to the Talmud, Rashi feels constrained to remark, "Even though [God] commanded [Abraham to offer his son] it did not enter [God's] mind that Abraham should slaughter him, for it was only to test [Abraham]." In any case, this Talmudic passage speaks powerfully to the paradoxical character of the Akeda when read in the context of all we know of Judaism's insistence upon the abominable character of the institution of human sacrifice.

As noted above, in the course of time and in consequence of the tragic history of the People of Israel, the Akeda became a paradigm for *Kiddush Hashem* – martyrdom. But in the context of the Torah's narrative, the Akeda is troubling, for it seems to grant approbation to the willingness to engage in a rite otherwise denounced as an abomination.

With the rise of the *Haskala*, or the Jewish modernization movement at the end of the eighteenth and in the nineteenth centuries, a new way of explaining the Akeda emerged. The Akeda was seen as a watershed dividing pagan consciousness and the new sensibility of the Torah. In this view, Abraham is being instructed that God does not want human sacrifice. But if this is the case, why does the angel tell Abraham after the fact, "Now I know that you revere God, not holding back your son, uniquely yours, from me?" If the point was to condemn sacrifice, Abraham should have been condemned.

A much more nuanced account is presented by the nineteenth century scholar Samuel David Luzatto. Luzatto argues that in a world in which human sacrifice was part of the conventional religious consciousness, the Torah's proscription of human sacrifice would not have been viewed as a sign of moral elevation at all. It would have been judged instead as a sign of Jewish half-heartedness, an inability to fully commit to the unreserved service of the God of Israel. Perhaps this explains the attraction this form of worship had for at least some Jews of First Temple times. In Luzatto's words:

> For the other nations would say to Israel, "In what way do you love your God?" Perhaps Israelites themselves would hold their religion in contempt because of this absence [of human sacrifice]. Therefore, God first put Abraham to the test (after knowing his heart and his ability to pass the test) in order that both Israelites and the other peoples would understand and recognize that such a deed and even more difficult deeds would not be too difficult for the true servants of God, (for example, the slaughter of an only child to

> elderly parents) if God were to ask. But the true God does not want such sacrifices and in fact abominates them.[33]

In this rendering, the Akeda serves not to affirm human sacrifice, but to affirm a readiness to serve God unreservedly according to the values revealed by God himself in his Torah. This returns us to the explanation of the Akeda presented in Rambam's *Moreh Nevukhim*. It is a paradigm concerning the extent of the love and reverence we are to have for God. The Torah makes unyielding demands upon the Jew for total obedience. But our obedience is to the commandments of God only. Judaism, at the end of the day, is not a half-hearted religion at all, but a religion in which total submission is given to the God of justice and decency.

33. פירוש שד"ל על חמישה חומשי תורה (הוצאת דביר, 1966), 92.

Chapter 13

Akeda: Postscript

PARASHAT VAYERA

"The ethical is the universal."[34] This truism serves as the introductory statement that the nineteenth century Christian philosopher Soren Kierkegaard states each time he explores three questions prompted by his bold, explosive reading of the Akeda in *Fear and Trembling*. He first asks, "Is there a teleological suspension of the ethical?"[35] In other words, is there a greater purpose that can allow the transcending of moral limitation and duty?

Secondly, "Is there an absolute duty to God,"[36] a duty that is self-contained and not subject to universal moral judgment? Finally, Kierkegaard asks whether it was defensible for Abraham to conceal his understanding from Sarah, Eliezer, and Isaac.[37]

Let us begin with the last question first. Exactly what could Abraham tell anyone about his intentions to sacrifice his beloved child Isaac? What set of criteria would make anything Abraham was planning to do understandable? As we have seen, the Midrash has Satan accuse Abraham of madness in his resolve to destroy the gift of his child and remind him that he will stand accused of murder when the deed is done. The best that Abraham

34. Soren Kierkegaard, *Fear and Trembling*, edited and translated by Howard V. Hong and Edna H. Hong. (Princeton University Press), 54.

35. Ibid.

36. Ibid., 68.

37. Ibid., 82.

(and Isaac) could do in response was to say "Nonetheless!" While this Midrash does not figure in Kierkegaard's book, this philosopher poses the same questions in a different way. He imagines a preacher being told by a parishioner that he intends to follow Abraham's example. The imagined preacher tells the man, "You despicable man, you scum of society, what devil has so possessed you that you want to murder your son?" The clear implication is that this same accusation can be directed at Abraham.[38]

In Euripides' play *Iphigenia at Aulis,* the hero Agamemnon is called upon to sacrifice his beloved daughter Iphigenia to the gods to assure Panhellenic victory in the war against Troy. However horrific the deed might be to us, it could be explained in the context of the classical world and the exigencies of war. It could even be explained to Iphigenia, the daughter. There was a context in which the deed, though terrifying, was noble. Agamemnon is Kierkegaard's model for the tragic hero who wishes more than anything else that he could protect his daughter. But a deeper duty compels him to sacrifice her nonetheless. This deeper duty is heartrending and terrible, but it can be articulated.[39]

Abraham's case is different because no reason for the sacrifice of Isaac can be articulated beyond saying that it was a test of Abraham's faith, which cannot be related to any moral purpose. In Kierkegaard's words, "it cannot be mediated into the universal." In this act, "Abraham does nothing for the universal and the purpose is hidden."[40]

This is the excruciating dilemma confronting us in this account of the Akeda. Again, in Kierkegaard's words, "Either the single individual can stand in absolute relation to the Absolute and, consequently, the ethical is not the highest or Abraham is lost."[41] For Kierkegaard, "faith is the highest passion in a person" and its demands transcend the ethical.

To be sure, ethical perfection, which reflects what is universally binding on humanity, is divine. One can aspire to be a "knight of faith" to use Kierkegaard's terminology, only after

38. Ibid., 28. 39. Ibid., 79. 40. Ibid., 71. 41. Ibid., 120.

attaining ethical perfection. But if one's duty to God were to be exhausted in ethical perfection, then God would vanish in that attainment.[42] Kierkegaard's "knight of faith" moves beyond the ethical after being called by God to engage in a lonely journey in a self-contained relationship to Him. Abraham is Kierkegaard's model for the "knight of faith."

The question we must now consider is whether this exegesis of the Akeda is satisfying. Is it really true that there is no broader context of values in which the Akeda can be understood? As Luzatto has reminded us, there is a historical context for the Akeda, which is, in one sense, parallel to the historical context of Agamemnon's readiness to sacrifice Iphigenia. We should not forget that the Torah had to warn the Israelites not to seek out the abominable rites of the Canaanites in which "they even burned up their sons and daughters" to their gods (*Devarim* 12:31). What cannot be denied is that these rites proved to be attractive for at least some paganized First Temple Jews, and it demonstrated, for them, commitment and devotion to their gods. As we have seen, for Luzatto, the Akeda served as a counter-polemic against human sacrifices, indicating that the first father of Israel was prepared to make any commitment to his God, no matter how difficult, when commanded. But God abominates such sacrifices, accepting in its place Abraham's gesture of agonizing obedience.

At this point let us consider two "modern" approaches to the Akeda that spring from purely Jewish sources – the approaches of Rav Chaim Soloveitchik of Brisk (Brest-Litovsk) and Rav Mordechai Yosef Leiner, the Izhibitza Rebbe.

Rav Chaim presents the dilemma facing Abraham on the morning of the command to take Isaac to the Land of Moriah in terms of a formal rule of Halakhic exegesis ascribed to Rabbi Ishmael that we recite each morning. According to the thirteenth rule, when we are confronted by two verses in the Torah that contradict each other, we must await a third verse that will reconcile the contradiction. Abraham was confronted by such a contradiction. On the one hand, Abraham was promised, "In Isaac will your seed be called," an assurance that Isaac would live and

42. Ibid., 68

be the second father of the promised nation (*B'reishit* 21:12). But he was then told, "Offer up [Isaac] as a burnt offering" (*B'reishit* 22:2). In Hebrew, the term for giving a burnt offering is העלהו – *ha'alehu*. Abraham proceeded to live with that contradiction in the faith that a third reconciling verse would be found to make sense of it all. That third verse emerged when God's angel told him to cease and desist. "Now I know that you revere God." As Rashi notes, the actual command to Abraham was העלהו, which certainly connotes burning a whole offering, but in strictly literal terms it means "to raise him up" (Commentary on *B'reishit* 22:2). That this literal but eccentric meaning proved to be the intended purpose could only become clear retrospectively after the agony of the trial of the Akeda. What was always at stake was the willingness to do whatever was actually commanded but not the actual bloody deed.

The Izhbitza Rebbe also focuses on the contradiction between the promise of posterity through Isaac and the command to offer him up as a burnt offering. He further mentions the obvious: that this would also violate the prohibition against murder.

But the Izhbitza does not attempt to escape the horns of the dilemma by referencing Rabbi Ishmael's thirteenth rule. Rather, he cites the *Zohar*, which notes the use of the Divine name E-lohim in the command (*B'reishit* 22:1). This name represents God's distance and the quality of Divine harsh judgment. In the *Zohar*'s words this means that this command comes to Abraham through "a darkened glass" that rendered everything confused (*Zohar* I 120). But Abraham proceeded in faith that the original promise of posterity through Isaac would somehow not be betrayed. The angel that stays Abraham's hand is called an angel of Y-H-V-H, a name that reflects God's closeness and clarity of vision.[43]

For Kierkegaard, a radical dichotomy is at work between universal ethical obligation and the lonely road of the "knight of faith" for whom the ethical has been transcended. By contrast, for both of these representatives of Rabbinic Judaism, the Mitnaged Rav Chaim and the Hassidic Izhbitza Rebbe, Abraham

43. מי השילוח Vol. I (ספרי קדש מישור), 19, 29.

trusts that an underlying ethical purpose in the command will be revealed in the course of time.

The Ashkenazic communities that stubbornly refused all surrender to the Crusaders and even slaughtered their own children to prevent their apostasy, were confronted with a moral dilemma in no way less excruciating than Abraham our father. They did not, for one moment, believe that they had transcended the ethical. They deeply believed that the justification for their deeds would be revealed in the course of time.

Chapter 14

Twice Given: The Land and the Child

PARASHAT CHAYEI SARAH

WHEN ABRAHAM BEGINS HIS ODYSSEY in *Parashat Lekh L'kha,* God tells him that he will be the founder of a great nation. Once in the designated land, he is further promised that the land will belong to his descendants. But all of this lies in the future. For now, Abraham can only describe himself to the inhabitants of Hebron as a "resident alien" (*B'reishit* 23:4). When Sarah dies, Abraham must secure the rights to a gravesite and negotiations begin with Ephron the Hittite in Hebron over purchase of the cave and field of Machpelah.

Ephron initially offers the site to Abraham as a gift but Abraham insists on paying the full price for the site. Ephron then responds, "My lord, listen to me. This land is worth 400 *shekalim*. Between you and me what is that? So bury your dead" (23:15).

How are we to understand Ephron's response? Rashi, following the Midrash *B'reishit Rabba,* says about Ephron, "He said much but did very little, taking 400 of the largest *shekalim,* each one equal to 100 *maneh*" (Commentary on 23:16).

However, one can read the conversation between the two men differently. Radak begins with Abraham's insistence on paying for the gravesite in full and refusing to accept the site as a gift. Ephron is only responding to that insistence. In effect, Ephron is saying, "If you insist on full payment, the price is 400 *shekalim*. But whether you pay me or not, by all means, bury your dead" (Commentary on *B'reishit* 23:16). In this reading, Ephron is being magnanimous throughout.

It is this explanation that better explains Abraham's motives in insisting on full payment. Abraham does not want to be forever in need of the magnanimity of others. He seeks unambiguous ownership, which will not only allow his own burial next to his wife, but will allow the Machpelah to be the burial place in the future for Isaac and Rebecca, and later, for Jacob and Leah. In this way, Abraham bequeaths a plot of land to future generations. A tomb is not only a burial place for one's ancestors. It can become the womb of the nation, guaranteeing a stake in the land to one's descendants and creating uncompromising yearning for that land.

Much later, when Israel stands at the cusp of entering the land, Moses will send twelve spies in preparation for conquest (*Bamidbar* 13:1–33, 14:1–10). Ten of the twelve will lose heart at the prospect for success and will bring back a disheartening report. But Joshua and Caleb are not disheartened and bravely seek to keep everyone's spirit high. Joshua was already known to us as Moses' disciple, but Caleb was not previously known to us. What set him apart from the other spies enabling him to rise above despair? The Talmud in *Sotah* says that Caleb alone went to Hebron to prostrate himself at the graves of his ancestors (34b). The graves of Israel's founders, unambiguously belonging to Israel, created the unbreakable attachment. In effect, the land is twice given to Abraham, first in God's promise and then in Abraham's purchase of the Machpelah.

After Sarah's burial, the Torah tells us, "Abraham was old, advanced in years. God had blessed Abraham in everything" (*B'reishit* 24:1). This "blessing in everything" is identified by Rashi with Isaac (Commentary on 24:1). If a stake in the land was twice given in both promise and purchase, Isaac was the twice given son, first in his miraculous birth and then after being tied down upon an altar and then released to new life in the aftermath of the Akeda. But as Rashi continues, this "blessing in everything" will be significant only if Isaac marries and has children.

Abraham then summons a servant that tradition identifies as Eliezer and instructs him to find an appropriate wife for Isaac.

Under no circumstances is Isaac to marry a Canaanite woman. Rather, the servant is sent to Aram-Naharaim, the land of Abraham's family. Furthermore, the servant is specifically told that under no circumstances is Isaac to leave the land, and therefore the selected woman must agree to come back to Canaan in order to marry Isaac (*B'reishit* 24:28). In fact, at no point will Isaac ever leave the land. Later, when there is another famine, God will pointedly forbid Isaac to follow his father's example in leaving for Egypt (*B'reishit* 26:1–2). For all of this, Abraham exacts an oath from his servant and instructs him to "place your hand under my thigh." What exactly is Abraham instructing the servant to do?

Ibn Ezra and Radak understand Abraham to be saying that the servant is to literally put his hand under Abraham's thigh while he sits, demonstrating the subservience of the servant's deeds to Abraham's person (Commentary on 24:2). However, Rashi, following *Midrash Rabba,* is undoubtedly correct when he understands the phrase "under my thigh" to be a euphemism for the genitals. In several places in Tanakh, descendants are referred to as יֹצְאֵי יְרֵכוֹ, "the issue of his thigh," clearly a euphemism for the genitals. The procreative power of the genitals is the one function of the human organism that can survive death and promise posterity. Specifically, Rashi says that the servant was to place his hand on the mark of circumcision on Abraham's phallus (Commentary on 24:2). The mark of circumcision is what consecrates Abraham's procreative power to a covenantal relationship to God and constitutes the first visible symbol of that relationship. Taken this way, the oath not only binds the servant to do his master's bidding. It informs his mission with responsibility for the continuation of the covenant.

But what human qualities beyond biological continuity and ownership of the land are to be transmitted through the covenant of Abraham? This becomes manifest in the way the servant conducts the search for the right partner for Isaac.

When the servant arrives at his destination in Aram-Naharaim, he sees many young women drawing water from a well. Which woman is he to consider? The servant prays for success in his mission and in his prayers he sets up a test. He will ask one young woman for some water. If she is generous and not only offers him water to drink, but also offers to draw water for his camels, then "she is the woman that God has chosen for my master's son" (*B'reishit* 24:10–14).

What is the point of this test? Rashi says that the servant was searching for character traits indicating kindness and generosity of spirit, traits summed up in the Hebrew word חסד – *hessed* (Commentary on 24:14). In fact, in the narrative of the finding of the right wife, the word חסד appears four times.

The servant finds this woman in Rebecca and wonders whether God has indeed led him to the right choice. In fact, she proves to be the granddaughter of Abraham's brother Nahor. The servant is welcomed to the family home by Laban, Rebecca's brother, and he secures Rebecca's hand in marriage for Isaac (*B'reishit* 23:24–61).

After the return journey and after the wedding, we are told, "Isaac takes Rebecca into the tent of Sarah his mother, taking her as his wife and loving her. Isaac then found comfort after Sarah's passing" (*B'reishit* 24:67).

That striking description of their marital relationship underscores the sense in which Isaac embodies the promise to Abraham of posterity "for in Isaac will your seed be called." Later the Torah will tell us that Isaac would redig the wellsprings of his father (*B'reishit* 26:18). Isaac then remains above all the "*ben berit*" – the child of the covenant upon which the servant swore to find an appropriate wife. The redigging of Abraham's wellsprings serves as a metaphor for the nature of Isaac's life and mission.

Isaac is a man of peace. At no point in the Torah's narrative does Isaac engage in warfare. When the servant returns from Aram-Naharaim with Rebecca, Isaac is himself returning from the wellspring of LaHai Roi, the very well that had served as a resting place for Hagar, Abraham's pregnant concubine, when she ran away from Sarah's persecutions. The Midrash suggests that after Sarah's death, Isaac had gone there to bring Hagar back to be reconciled with his father Abraham (*B'reishit Rabba* 60:14).

Whether or not that Midrash captures the actual motivations

of Isaac in going to LaHai Roi, it is striking that when Abraham dies, both Isaac and Hagar's son Ishmael bury their father together in the Machpelah gravesite where Sarah had been buried. Isaac, the second father of Israel, then lives the rest of his life in the land promised to Abraham.

Chapter 15

Oracles and Destiny

PARASHAT TOLDOT

LIKE ABRAHAM AND SARAH BEFORE THEM, Isaac and Rebecca are initially childless. They pray and after twenty years, Rebecca conceives and will give birth to twins. But during the pregnancy, Rebecca senses a struggle ensuing in her womb, and she seeks Divine explanation of her sufferings (*B'reishit* 25:19–22). She receives the following oracle:

Two nations are in your womb	שְׁנֵי גֹיִים בְּבִטְנֵךְ
Two peoples will separate from your body	וּשְׁנֵי לְאֻמִּים מִמֵּעַיִךְ יִפָּרֵדוּ
One people will struggle with the other,	וּלְאֹם מִלְאֹם יֶאֱמָץ
And the older shall serve the younger.	וְרַב יַעֲבֹד צָעִיר
(*B'reishit* 25:23)	

It is critical to note that this oracle is received by Rebecca alone, and Isaac is apparently never apprised of its contents.

When the children are born, it is the first of the twins that appears remarkable; he is ruddy and covered with hair (*B'reishit* 25:25). The ruddiness of the baby speaks to his robustness, and his hairiness is a premonition of virility and power. David, the first king of Israel, was ruddy, and Samson's virile power was conferred through the growth of his hair. The child is named עשו – Essau, and Rashi suggests that the name means that he was עשוי, "completed," as if already pubescent (Commentary on *B'reishit* 25:25).

By contrast, the second of the twins is physically unremarkable except that, ominously, his hand is holding fast to his brother's heel. For this reason, he is named יעקב – Jacob, which plays upon the Hebrew word עקב – *akev*, or "heel" (*B'reishit* 25:26). The two children grow and Essau becomes a hunter, "a man of the field," whereas Jacob is described as a "mild man who dwells in tents."

Isaac especially loves Essau, the hunter, whose captured game he enjoyed. We should also note that as the oldest, Essau was entitled to the birthright in the normal course of things. But Rebecca favors Jacob who, according to the oracle given exclusively to her, is destined to be preeminent (*B'reishit* 25:27–28).

The Torah now sets the stage for the unfolding rivalry between the brothers and depicts their contrasting characteristics. One day, Jacob is cooking a lentil stew when Essau returns from the hunt tired and ravenously hungry. Rashi cites a rabbinic tradition that says that Abraham had died on that day, and Jacob was preparing the meal of condolence (Commentary on *B'reishit* 25:30). However, Radak captures the plain sense of the narrative by saying that Jacob was simply cooking a meal for himself, which means that Jacob, too, was hungry, even if not as famished as his brother (Commentary on *B'reishit* 25:29).

Essau turns to his brother and says:

> הַלְעִיטֵנִי נָא מִן הָאָדֹם הָאָדֹם הַזֶּה כִּי עָיֵף אָנֹכִי
> Stuff me with that red, red stuff because I am famished. (*B'reishit* 25:30)

The language is blatantly crude. The Mishna in Tractate *Shabbat* employs the same verb הלעטה – *ha'alata* for placing food into the mouth of a camel (24:3). There is crudity also in the reference to the stew as "red, red stuff." As Rashi puts it, it is as if Essau is saying, "I will open my mouth as you pour into it" (Commentary on *B'reishit* 25:30).

Derisively, the Torah, alluding to the people that will emerge from Essau, Edom (which means "red"), says, "that is why they call his name Edom" (*B'reishit* 25:30). Jacob turns to his brother and says, "Then, right now, sell me your birthright." Essau responds, "I am about to die. Of what use is my birthright?" Now we can certainly understand that Essau was extremely hungry, but imminent death was not likely. When Jacob demands an oath, Essau readily complies and sells his birthright to his brother for the proverbial "mess of pottage."

Now, following Radak, Jacob was also hungry. But Jacob was prepared to forgo the instant gratification of a full belly for a birthright that would be realized only in the distant future. Essau, by contrast, is prepared to sacrifice future promise for the pleasure of the moment. Essau fills his stomach and the Torah then says about Essau, "He ate, he drank, he rose, and he went, for Essau despised the birthright" (*B'reishit* 25:31–33). The staccato effect of the words describing Essau's behavior captures the simple-minded boorishness of the man.

By contrast, Jacob is reflective and calculating; he understands the birthright's value and is willing to sacrifice for it. Later Essau will take not one but two Canaanite wives, embittering the spirits of his parents (*B'reishit* 26:34). Impulse control is not his strong suit. The stage has been set for the climactic drama. Isaac becomes old and infirm and his eyesight has dimmed. In spite of Essau's troubling marriages, Isaac is determined to bestow the blessing of preeminence upon him. His physical blindness serves as a metaphor for his blindness to Essau's unworthiness (*B'reishit* 27:1–4).

Now this bestowal of blessing is portrayed in almost sacramental terms. The blessing is to be given "before God" and in the context of a celebratory meal that Essau is to prepare from the game he has hunted. Once pronounced, it cannot be revoked (*B'reishit* 27:33). Essau sets out on his mission.

Rebecca overhears Isaac's instructions to Essau but is determined that it will be Jacob, not Essau, who will be blessed. She cajoles the reluctant Jacob to engage in an elaborate subterfuge to secure the blessing intended for Essau. She instructs him to bring two kids from the flock that she will cook and doctor to the taste Isaac anticipates from Essau's hunt. Rebecca covers Jacob's smooth arms with the goat hair to simulate hairiness and she clothes Jacob in Essau's celebratory garments. When Jacob enters Isaac's quarters with the prepared food pretending to be Essau, Isaac suspects something is amiss. He feels Jacob's disguised arms and remarks:

> הַקֹּל קוֹל יַעֲקֹב וְהַיָּדַיִם יְדֵי עֵשָׂו
> The voice is the voice of Jacob, but the hands are the hands of Essau. (*B'reishit* 27:22)

That one phrase captures the theme of the sibling rivalry. The narrative projects a struggle between two distinct forces. Essau embodies brute strength and instinctual power, the powers of the fist. These qualities are by no means unimportant to a productive life. The Talmud remarks, "Whoever is greater than his fellow has urges equally more powerful" (Tractate *Succah* 52a). Perhaps Isaac imagined that such qualities were of primary importance in laying building blocks for the future nation destined to emerge from his loins. By contrast, Jacob embodies the force represented by the voice – articulation and reflection, qualities residing in the mind rather than the blood.

In spite of initial suspicions, Isaac is sufficiently convinced to invest blessing in the son standing before him. The deception succeeds and Jacob steals the blessing intended for Essau.

When Essau arrives with his game carefully prepared for his father, the moment of truth leaves Isaac in a state of turmoil. "Who then was it that hunted game and brought it to me? Moreover I ate it before you came and I blessed him. He shall then be blessed!" (*B'reishit* 27:30–33). Essau begins to cry bitterly and wildly. But it is all too late. "Your brother came with deception and took your blessing" (*B'reishit* 27:35). Enraged, Essau exclaims:

> וַיֹּאמֶר הֲכִי קָרָא שְׁמוֹ יַעֲקֹב וַיַּעְקְבֵנִי זֶה פַעֲמַיִם אֶת בְּכֹרָתִי לָקָח וְהִנֵּה עַתָּה לָקַח בִּרְכָתִי
> It is fitting that his name is *Jacob*, for he *tricked* me twice. He took my *birthright* and now he took my *blessing*. (*B'reishit* 27:36)

Essau settles on a second explanation for Jacob's name. Not only does עקב – *akev* mean heel, but it can also imply trickery. How fitting then is Jacob's name! But there is another word play in Essau's statement that Essau does not consider. The Hebrew word for "blessing" is ברכה – *b'rakha*. The word for birthright is בכרה – *b'khora*. A simple inversion of the Hebrew letter כ with the letter ר is the entire difference between blessing and birthright. Blessing and birthright are two sides of the same coin. Forfeiture of the birthright is what led to the forfeiture of the blessing.

To be sure, none of this changes the fact that Jacob, however prodded by his mother, deceived his father and took advantage of his father's infirmity to take something Isaac intended for Jacob's brother.

Centuries later, during the last days of the First Temple in Jerusalem, when the prophet Jeremiah denounces the tragic corruption of Jewish society at that time, he will say:

> אִישׁ מֵרֵעֵהוּ הִשָּׁמֵרוּ וְעַל־כָּל אָח אַל תִּבְטָחוּ כִּי כָל אָח עָקוֹב יַעְקֹב וְכָל רֵעַ רָכִיל יַהֲלֹךְ׃
>
> Let each man be on guard with his neighbor, let no one trust his brother, for each *brother is deceitful*, every neighbor bears tales. (Jeremiah 9:3)

In Hebrew, it is possible to read the italicized phrase as "for every brother behaves as Jacob!"

The moral thread that weaves through the Torah's narrative will not allow this outrage to pass without cost. Jacob will, in time, pay dearly for this deception. But at this point, the Torah is content to contrast the relative value of physical prowess and instinctual power measured against personal restraint and intelligence, and the Torah celebrates the latter. As Midrash *B'reishit Rabba* puts it: "Jacob only rules with his voice. Essau only rules with his hands" (45:20). And the voice vanquishes the fist.

But let us consider the actual words of the blessing over which the struggle was waged.

> וְיִתֶּן לְךָ אֱ־לֹהִים מִטַּל הַשָּׁמַיִם וּמִשְׁמַנֵּי הָאָרֶץ וְרֹב דָּגָן וְתִירֹשׁ יַעַבְדוּךָ עַמִּים וְיִשְׁתַּחֲוּוּ לְךָ לְאֻמִּים הֱוֵה גְבִיר לְאַחֶיךָ וְיִשְׁתַּחֲווּ לְךָ בְּנֵי אִמֶּךָ אֹרְרֶיךָ אָרוּר וּמְבָרְכֶיךָ בָּרוּךְ׃
>
> May God give you of the dew of heaven and of the fat of

> the earth with abundant grain and wine. Nations will serve you, peoples will bow to you. Be preeminent over your brethren, may your mother's children bow to you. May those who curse you be cursed, those who bless you be blessed. (*B'reishit* 27:28–29)

What is most striking about this blessing is that it is a blessing of riches, power, and preeminence, but devoid of obvious spiritual or moral content.

Essau pleads for at least one blessing from his father. Isaac provides a compensatory blessing to Essau of the riches of the earth and dew of the heavens. Then he tells his crestfallen first-born son, "you will live by your sword and serve your brother. But when you grow restive, you shall break his yoke from your neck" (*B'reishit* 27:40).

The furious Essau prepares to kill his brother once his father dies. Sensing this, Rebecca urges Jacob to flee to her brother Laban in Haran until Essau's anger subsides. The ever-wily Rebecca tells her husband that she cannot bear Essau's Canaanite wives and asks Isaac to send Jacob to Haran to find an appropriate wife among their kinsmen. Now Isaac blesses Jacob a second time before he departs.

> וְאֵ־ל שַׁ־דַּי יְבָרֵךְ אֹתְךָ וְיַפְרְךָ וְיַרְבֶּךָ וְהָיִיתָ לִקְהַל עַמִּים. וְיִתֶּן לְךָ אֶת בִּרְכַּת אַבְרָהָם לְךָ וּלְזַרְעֲךָ אִתָּךְ לְרִשְׁתְּךָ אֶת אֶרֶץ מְגֻרֶיךָ אֲשֶׁר נָתַן אֱ־לֹהִים לְאַבְרָהָם.
> May E-l Sha-dai bless you, make you fruitful that you multiply and become a community of nations. May He grant the blessing of Abraham to you and your seed after you that you inherit the land of your dwelling that God gave to Abraham. (*B'reishit* 28:3–4)

What does this blessing add to the blessing over which Jacob and Essau became such bitter rivals? First the Divine name used is E-l Sha-dai, the name God uses when he gives the Covenant of Circumcision to Abraham. This is only the second time this Divine name appears in the Torah. As noted in the discussions on Lekh L'kha, in Genesis this name always appears in the context of reproduction and the consecration of reproductive power to God. This blessing talks explicitly about the Promised Land and the legacy of Abraham. The first blessing was about riches, preeminence, and power, and we can understand why Essau would have wanted it. This blessing is about the covenant of Abraham. It will ultimately be important only to Jacob.

Chapter 16

A Midrashic Postscript

PARASHAT TOLDOT

WHEN ADAM AND EVE SIN and are confronted by God with the consequences of their deed, The Torah tells us that God himself fashions garments of skin for them and clothes them (*B'reishit* 3:21). According to a Midrashic tradition, these fabulous garments are taken into the ark by Noah and thus survive the great flood (*Pirkei R' Eliezer* 24). Ham, the son of Noah, who was cursed by his father, misappropriates these garments and they become the inheritance of Nimrod his grandson. When Nimrod clothes himself in these garments of the first human being, all the beasts of the field and birds of the sky bow down to him, and this is what the Torah means when it says about Nimrod, "He was a mighty hunter before God" (*B'reishit* 10:9).

Now just as Nimrod was a hunter, so was Essau. One day, Essau goes out to hunt and finds Nimrod. The two predators confront each other, and Essau kills Nimrod and seizes these fabulous garments, which now become his possession. These then, are the בִּגְדֵי חֲמוּדוֹת – the celebratory garments that Rebecca surreptitiously gives to Jacob as part of the disguise that will enable him to seize Isaac's blessing intended for Essau (*B'reishit* 27:15). In Hebrew the word חמד – *hamod*, here translated as "celebratory," can also mean "coveted," as in לא תחמוד – "you shall not covet." Coveting becomes especially egregious if it leads to illegal seizure. That is what has happened to these magical garments.

When Jacob approaches his father in this disguise, Isaac smells those garments, and the Torah says, "He smelled the scent of his garments and he blessed him saying, 'Ah, the scent of my son is like the scent of the field God has blessed'" (*B'reishit* 27:27). According to this tradition, this scent was the scent of the Garden of Eden where these garments were fashioned (*B'reishit Rabba* 65:22).

It would be unfortunate indeed if one misses the point by focusing upon the details of the story instead of its deeper meaning. In this Midrashic retelling of the story, the Divinely given regal garments of humanity were misappropriated by the family of Nimrod who, as "a mighty hunter," represents the predatory forces within humanity.[44] Essau represents that same predatory tendency. When Rebecca takes those garments, she is reclaiming the regal garments of humanity for the forces of mind and spirit. When Isaac's blessings descend upon Jacob adorned in those garments, a new and positive turn in human destiny has been taken. Mind and spirit, "the voice of Jacob," have been restored to their rightful place. The garments have been restored to what is best in humanity.

44. Yitzhak Danciger's sculpture of Nimrod, on view at the Israel Museum, so controversial in its time (1939), provides us with a picture of Nimrod and all that he represents in Midrashic tradition. Nimrod stands naked with his genitals fully sculpted, and he is uncircumcised. He carries his bow on his back and it seemingly serves as his backbone. In other words, his tools of violence are what define him as a man.

Chapter 17

Jacob: Faith and Skepticism

PARASHAT VAYETZEI

At the end of Parashat Toldot, Rebecca urges Jacob to flee to her family in Haran to escape Essau's murderous anger. Isaac, presumably, knows nothing of Essau's intentions and Rebecca does not tell him. However, she does convince him to send Jacob to Haran – but for a different reason. Essau had embittered his parents' lives with his choice of Canaanite (or Hittite) wives. She asks her husband to let Jacob go to Haran and there he will marry appropriately (*B'reishit* 27:42–28:9).

As we have seen, Isaac's final blessing, before Jacob's departure, bestows upon him the life missions of Abraham and Isaac. But Jacob's immediate concern is to escape his brother's wrath. When nightfall descends upon him, he must lie down alone with only a hard stone for a pillow. This barren stone is emblematic of Jacob's forlorn condition.

But as Jacob sleeps, he has a wondrous dream that paints a very different picture of Jacob's present reality. From the location where he sleeps there is a ladder mounted upon the earth and reaching upward to the heavens. Angels of God are ascending and descending upon it, and the Torah says, וְהִנֵּה ה' נִצָּב עָלָיו, which means that God is standing either above or upon the ladder's highest rung, or above or beside Jacob (*B'reishit* 28:10–13). In any case, in his dream, Jacob is not alone at all; he is in the company of God and His angels, and a ladder is connecting heaven and earth.

God now addresses Jacob:

> וַיֹּאמַר אֲנִי ה׳ אֱ־לֹהֵי אַבְרָהָם אָבִיךָ וֵא־לֹהֵי יִצְחָק הָאָרֶץ אֲשֶׁר אַתָּה שֹׁכֵב עָלֶיהָ לְךָ אֶתְּנֶנָּה וּלְזַרְעֶךָ. וְהָיָה זַרְעֲךָ כַּעֲפַר הָאָרֶץ וּפָרַצְתָּ יָמָּה וָקֵדְמָה וְצָפֹנָה וָנֶגְבָּה וְנִבְרְכוּ בְךָ כָּל מִשְׁפְּחֹת הָאֲדָמָה וּבְזַרְעֶךָ. וְהִנֵּה אָנֹכִי עִמָּךְ וּשְׁמַרְתִּיךָ בְּכֹל אֲשֶׁר תֵּלֵךְ וַהֲשִׁבֹתִיךָ אֶל הָאֲדָמָה הַזֹּאת כִּי לֹא אֶעֱזָבְךָ עַד אֲשֶׁר אִם עָשִׂיתִי אֵת אֲשֶׁר דִּבַּרְתִּי לָךְ.
>
> I am Y-H-V-H, the God of your father Abraham and the God of Isaac. The land upon which you lie will I give you and your seed. Your descendants will be as the dust of the earth. You shall burst forth to the west and the east, the north and the south. In you and in your descendants will all the families of the earth be blessed. I will be with you and protect you whenever you go. Then I will bring you back to this land. I will not leave you until I have done all that I have told you. (*B'reishit* 28:13–15)

When Jacob awakes, he awakens to the same desolate reality he found when he lay down to sleep, but his dream has expanded his sense of reality. He says, "Surely God is in this place and I was unaware [of that fact.]" Trepidation fills him and he says, "How awesome is this place! This is none other than the House of God; it is the gate of heaven" (*B'reishit* 28:16–17). In other words, Jacob is not really alone, but in the company of God and angels. God has now confirmed that Jacob will indeed bear the destiny of Abraham and Isaac within him. Jacob's descendants will inherit the Promised Land, and through them God's blessing will encompass all nations. Jacob left home a fugitive from his brother's murderous intent, but now he has been assured of God's protective guidance. With this assurance in hand he takes that sterile stone that he had used for a pillow and sets it up as a sacramental pillar. He anoints it and consecrates it to God. He calls the place where he slept Bet-El, which means House of God. But now Jacob makes a strikingly equivocal vow:

> אִם יִהְיֶה אֱ־לֹהִים עִמָּדִי וּשְׁמָרַנִי בַּדֶּרֶךְ הַזֶּה אֲשֶׁר אָנֹכִי הוֹלֵךְ וְנָתַן לִי לֶחֶם לֶאֱכֹל וּבֶגֶד לִלְבֹּשׁ. וְשַׁבְתִּי בְשָׁלוֹם אֶל בֵּית אָבִי וְהָיָה ה׳ לִי לֵא־לֹהִים. וְהָאֶבֶן הַזֹּאת אֲשֶׁר שַׂמְתִּי מַצֵּבָה יִהְיֶה בֵּית אֱ־לֹהִים וְכֹל אֲשֶׁר תִּתֶּן לִי עַשֵּׂר אֲעַשְּׂרֶנּוּ לָךְ.
>
> If God remains with me, if He protects me on the journey I

> am taking, and gives me bread to eat and clothing to wear and I return in safety to my father's house, *then* Y-H-V-H will be my God, and the stone I have erected as a pillar shall be the House of God and I will set aside a tithe for You. (*B'reishit* 28:20–22)

Ramban understands this to mean that Jacob's vow to God is conditional, and his acknowledgement of Y-H-V-H as his God is also conditional (Commentary on *B'reishit* 28:21). Only if God provides his needs and returns him in safety to his father's house will Y-H-V-H be his God. While Ramban gives this condition a deeper esoteric meaning, the plain sense is that Jacob is hedging his devotional bets. Jacob is not only a reflective man; he is a prudent man. His initial overwhelming awareness and reverence is now tempered with caution. At this point, Jacob is a man in whom faith and doubt confront each other. (This will change later.) His original bifurcated purpose, flight to merely survive on the one hand and bearing the destiny of Abraham on the other, returns in force.

The sages say, "A dream that is not interpreted is like a letter unread" (Tractate *B'rakhot* 55a). Let us consider the visual symbols in Jacob's dream. Rashi follows a Midrashic tradition that says that the ascending angels on the ladder are the angels of Eretz Yisrael, and the descending angels are the angels of exile. As Jacob leaves the land, he is to be accompanied by a different angelic dispensation (Commentary on *B'reishit* 28:12). Rambam understands the ladder and its angels to represent the totality of the cosmos governed by God through the agency of the natural order (*Moreh Nevukhim* II 10). For Ramban, the ladder represents Israel's progression through history, with the angels representing oppressive empires that will rule until the Messianic redemption and the kingdom of God on earth (Commentary on *B'reishit* 28:12).

But there is a Midrashic tradition cited by Radak that draws a parallel between the revelation to Jacob in this dream and the revelation at Sinai (Commentary on *B'reishit* 28:12-13; *B'reishit Rabba* 68:12). The Midrash calls our attention to the coincidence of the numerical value of the word סלם, "ladder," with the numerical value of the name סיני – Sinai (130 in both cases). While the gematria itself need not concern us, the analogy between the two revelations is arresting.

At first glance, these two revelations are entirely different. In Jacob's dream, he is being assured of God's protection as he flees to Haran. At Sinai, God and Israel enact a covenant, God pronounces the Ten Articles of the Covenant (or Ten Commandments), and Israel is given a Torah. But we should consider the following.

No one needs a ladder unless there is an irreducible gap that must be bridged. A gap separates heaven, the realm of God, and the earth that has been given to men (Psalms 116:15). The distinction can never be dissolved, but only bridged. This Jacob sees in his dream.

In the covenant of Sinai, it is God's Torah that will bridge the gap between God and man. When the Mishkan, or desert sanctuary, is erected, the holy ark that will contain the stone tablets bearing the Ten Articles of the Covenant that serve as the preamble for the Torah's commandments, will be placed in the inner sanctum of this sanctuary. Above these tablets and as part of the covering of the ark, two carved angelic beings stand facing each other, their wings spread above their heads and forming a symbolic throne for an invisible Presence above (*Sh'mot* 25:10–22). God, then, is enthroned over His words. In Tractate *Succah*, the sages tell us that there were ten handbreadths from the top of the ark to the spread wings of the angelic cherubim. We are told that the minimum height of a kosher Succah is also ten handbreadths. Rashi explains that in both cases, ten handbreadths form a "disjunction of realms." In the case of the ark, the ten handbreadths are emblematic of the irreducible gap between God and man (*Succah* 5a–b, Rashi ad locum 5a). The sages go on to say that God's descent upon Mount Sinai retained the symbolic ten-handbreadth distance. Then, both at Sinai and in Jacob's dream, a gap between the Divine and the human always remains. This gap is the locus of both faith and doubt.

With doubt, there is no ladder and there are no ascending and descending angels to bridge the gap. The ladder and the angels represent faith. Awake, Jacob only knows the gap and its desolation, represented by the stone upon which he lays his head. Only in a dream do the ladder, its angelic denizens, and the Presence of God come into focus. Jacob's prudent caution lies in the discrepancy between what he sees while awake and what he sees when he dreams. Jacob's continuing story will be the story of triumph of faith over doubt.

Chapter 18

Measure for Measure: Jacob, Rachel, and Leah

PARASHAT VAYETZEI

WHATEVER DOUBTS JACOB MAY HAVE HARBORED at Bet-El, or Bethel, the content of his dream has buoyed him, and with enthusiasm and purpose, "Jacob lifts up his feet and travels to the land of the easterners" (*B'reishit* 29:1 and commentaries of Rashi, Rashbam, Radak, Seforno ad locum). When he reaches Haran, he sees a well covered by a large rock. Three flocks of sheep are resting next to it and the shepherds are idle. Jacob questions their idleness and the shepherds explain that they must wait for all the shepherds to gather, for they will need their collective strength to roll away the rock covering the well. He asks them if they know his uncle, Laban. They acknowledge that they do and they point toward his beautiful daughter, Rachel, who is just now coming to the well to water her father's sheep. When Jacob sees Rachel, he is overwhelmed and he single-handedly rolls away the rock, waters her sheep, kisses her, and begins to weep.

Rachel in turn runs to tell her father of their kinsman's arrival. Laban comes to greet Jacob; he embraces him and welcomes Jacob into his home (*B'reishit* 29:1–14).

Jacob remains at their home for a month until Laban makes it clear that he expects Jacob to work for him. With very little subtlety, Laban says to Jacob, "Just because you are a kinsman, should that mean that you should work for nothing? Name your wages" (*B'reishit* 29:15).

Now the Torah tells us that Laban had two daughters; Leah

was the older and Rachel the younger. Rachel is described as beautiful in face and shape. With regard to Leah, we are told only that her eyes were רכות – *rakot*. Radak understands this ambiguous word to mean weepy and tender. On the other hand, Rav Sa'adia Gaon and Rashbam understand this word to mean that her eyes were gentle and lovely. As the sages say, "A bride whose eyes are beautiful requires no further investigation" (*Ta'anit* 24a).

In any case, Jacob has fallen in love with Rachel and he offers to work for seven years to obtain her hand in marriage. Laban's somewhat equivocal reply is that "it is better for me to give her to you than another, so remain with me" (*B'reishit* 29:18–19).

Now the Midrash *B'reishit Rabba* reminds us that just as Isaac had two sons, so did Laban have two daughters. This Midrash goes on to tell us that people would say that Leah, Laban's eldest daughter, was destined to marry Essau, Isaac's eldest son, and Jacob, Isaac's younger son, would marry Rachel. That prediction caused Leah to constantly weep until her eyes became weak with the tears she shed (*B'reishit Rabba* 70:16). This Midrash is focusing upon a subtle thread connecting the Torah's narratives.

The Torah now tells us that the seven years of labor seemed to fly by for Jacob, so great was his love for Rachel (*B'reishit* 29:14–21). Finally, the time for the marriage arrives, and Jacob turns to his father-in-law to-be and says, "Give me my wife. I have fulfilled my service and I want to have relations with her" (*B'reishit* 29:21). As Rashi comments, following the Midrash, even the crudest person would hesitate to put the matter quite that way, especially to his father-in-law. However, we should note that we have already met one crude person who does talk in this manner. Essau talks this way, and once in his youth, when Essau was filled with a different physical need, he gave away his birthright for a mess of pottage.

Without reference to Jacob's crudity, Laban prepares a wedding feast. But that night, he brings a veiled Leah to Jacob instead of Rachel. The unsuspecting groom consummates a marriage with her.

In the morning, Jacob awakes and sees Leah beside him in place of his beloved. The furious groom confronts his father-in-law and says, "What did you do to me? I worked for Rachel! למה רמיתני, Why did you deceive me?" (*B'reishit* 29:22–25). Now the word רמיתני – *remitani*, "for you deceived me," has the same root as מרמה – *mirma*, which is the word Isaac used at the moment of truth when he had to tell Essau, "Your brother came with מרמה, deception, and took your blessing" (*B'reishit* 27:35).

Laban retorts, "It is not done in our place to give the younger before the older" (*B'reishit* 29:26). To put it another way, "I don't know what they do in *your* place. Perhaps in Canaan you can give the birthright to the younger child rather than the older, but not here! Jacob, you wanted the portion of the elder child. You have received it. You have received Leah."

Precisely when Jacob lowers his guard, allows instinct to overwhelm his judgment so that he speaks as crudely as his brother Essau, he receives his comeuppance. Moreover, just as Jacob deceived his father when his eyes were dim, he in turn is deceived by a woman whose eyes are tender. In this way the Torah weaves its moral thread through the narrative fabric. Even Jacob, or perhaps especially Jacob, third father of the promised nation, must pay a stiff price for moral turpitude. After the seven days of the wedding celebration, Laban will allow Jacob to marry Rachel as well, but he will have to work for seven more years. Needless to say, even though Laban is instrumental for punishing Jacob's moral lapse, he is hardly a saint. It is rather that Jacob has met his match in Laban.

Jacob's now polygamous marital state will produce its own bitter fruit. "God sees that Leah is resented. He opens her womb while Rachel remains barren" (*B'reishit* 29:31). The names Leah gives to her first four children speak to the pathos of her situation. She calls her firstborn, Reuben – "See, a son, for God has seen my agony. Now my husband will love me" (*B'reishit* 29:32). She calls her second child Simeon "for God has been attentive to my resented state" (*B'reishit* 29:33). She has a third son and calls him Levi, which means accompaniment "because now my husband will accompany me" (*B'reishit* 29:34). Hizkuni comments that with two toddlers and a baby, she will need her husband to walk with the first two children while she holds the baby (Commentary ad locum). When her fourth child is born,

Leah, the initially resented co-wife, is triumphant, certain of her indispensability to her husband. She names the child Judah, for "now I will thank God" (*B'reishit* 29:35).

Now Rachel is in despair for she remains barren. She turns to Jacob and pleads, "Give me children or I shall die." But Jacob lashes out at the love of his life. "Am I in God's place, who deprived you of a fruitful womb?" (*B'reishit* 30:1–2). The sages comment on this insensitive retort. "Is it appropriate to answer one who suffers in this manner? As you live, Jacob, your other children will have to stand in the presence of her (yet to be born) son" (*B'reishit Rabba* 71:7). But that will occur much later. At this point, a desperate Rachel prevails upon Jacob to bed her maidservant Bilhah, so that through her, Rachel might have surrogate children. When Leah senses that her fecundity has come to an end, she also insists that Jacob bed her maidservant, Zilpah, and four children will be born to the two servant women (*B'reishit* 30:3–11). But this surrogacy does not satisfy Rachel's yearnings.

One day, during the harvest season, Leah's son Reuben finds mandrakes growing in the field and he takes them to his mother. It was commonly believed at the time that these herbs have aphrodisiac and reproductive powers (Commentaries of Ibn Ezra, Radak, and Ramban on *B'reishit* 30:14). When Rachel sees them, she asks her sister, "Please give me some of your son's mandrakes." An angry Leah responds, "Is it not enough that you have taken my husband? Do you also need to take my son's mandrakes?" Rachel then says, "He will lie with you tonight in exchange for your son's mandrakes." When Jacob returns from work in the evening, Leah goes to greet him and tells him, "You will come with me for I have hired you in exchange for my son's mandrakes" (*B'reishit* 30:14–16). This episode not only records the depth of enmity and pathos of these women, but also serves to underscore the futility of folk medicine in the face of the Divine decree. Jacob indeed has relations with Leah that night, and she conceives a fifth son. She then gives birth to a sixth son and a daughter as well, while Rachel, though armed with the mandrakes, remains barren. After the birth of Leah's seventh child, God finally opens Rachel's womb and she gives birth to a son, causing her to say, "God has gathered away my shame."

She calls the child יוסף – Joseph, which not only sounds like the Hebrew word אסף, "gathers," but it also means to increase or add. Rachel prays, "May God add another son to me" (*B'reishit* 30:23–24). That will occur later when she gives birth to Benjamin.

As the story will tell us later, the painful rivalry of the two sisters and co-wives will continue into the next generation. Leah's children will sell Joseph, Rachel's son, into slavery. In the celebrated Midrashic tradition of the Ten Martyrs enshrined in the liturgy of both Yom Kippur and Tisha B'Av, a Roman oppressor will murder ten pure and holy sages with the excuse that he is exacting justice for the sale of Joseph by ten of his brothers back in the patriarchal period. This remarkable tradition will thus tie the tragedies of all of Jewish history to the rivalry of Rachel and Leah, Joseph and his brothers. It is as if fratricidal hatred and its consequences are embedded in our own national narrative.

But let us remember also that Laban justified his deception of Jacob, causing him to marry Leah before marrying Rachel, by obliquely referring back to Jacob's deception of his father and his brother Essau. The *Zohar* tells us that because of the tears that Essau shed when he understood what Jacob had done to him, Israel has shed tears under Essau's dominion through the long period of the exile (*Zohar* I 146a–b). All of this is the bitter harvest of deception.

Chapter 19

Jacob: Exile and Return

PARASHAT VAYETZEI

After the birth of Joseph, Jacob approaches his father-in-law Laban for permission to return with his now large family to his homeland. Laban acknowledges that Jacob's services have brought him extraordinary material success and he tells Jacob to designate appropriate compensation (*B'reishit* 30:25–28).

When Jacob first began to work for Laban fourteen years earlier, Laban had also asked Jacob to designate his wages. When Jacob asked for Rachel's hand in marriage as payment for seven years of labor, Laban then tricked him, switching Leah for Rachel on the wedding night and demanding seven more years of labor to "pay" for Rachel's hand. Certainly, at this point, Jacob knows with whom he is dealing and he proceeds cautiously and craftily. He reiterates what Laban has admitted about his contribution to Laban's wealth. In so many words, Jacob tells Laban to give him nothing at this point. Rather, Jacob will return to the task of tending Laban's flocks, and Jacob's wages will consist of goats that will be born from this point on that are spotted and streaked and sheep with dark markings. Laban is delighted, and just to be sure that very few goats and sheep with these characteristics are actually born from this point, he removes the male goats that are ringed and streaked, the female goats that are spotted and streaked, and every darkened sheep, and places them in the charge of his sons. Jacob is left with white monochromatic sheep and dark monochromatic goats (*B'reishit* 30:31–35).

Now Jacob has a plan. He prepares a place by the water troughs for the mating of animals he will select. First, Jacob marks this place with shoots of poplar, almond, and plane trees. He now strips part of the bark, producing white strips of wood beneath. It should be noted, at this point, that the name לבן – Laban, means "white" in Hebrew.

The place of mating is also designed to give the mating animals a view of the spotted and speckled animals already segregated by Laban's sons. The actual purpose of this elaborate ritual is obscure, though it reflects the actual practice of the Middle Eastern shepherds down to the present day. Perhaps it was only a ruse intended to hide from Laban what Jacob will now do. Jacob now separates the more vigorous animals from the weaker and breeds them separately (*B'reishit* 30:37–42). The Israeli scholar Yehuda Feliks has noted that this reproductive vigor is an indicator of the presence of recessive genes for spotted and speckled. By identifying this characteristic of heterosis or hybrid vigor and breeding these animals separately, Jacob is able to produce offspring that are spotted and speckled from animals that are ostensibly white. Feliks speculates that using this technique, Jacob was able to procure about 50% of Laban's flock on the first year.[45] Later it will become clear that Jacob's understanding of this technique that he employs was revealed to him in an angelic illumination (*B'reishit* 31:10–12).

White is a symbol of moral uprightness. Just as Laban, whose name means "white," disguises his darker qualities beneath a cloak of respectability, so too his white sheep disguise spotted characteristics within them. In effect, the Torah is telling us that Jacob is now defeating Laban at his own game, while following his agreement with Laban to the letter. Jacob now becomes a wealthy man (*B'reishit* 30:43).

There is now hostility with Laban's sons who murmur that Jacob has misappropriated property rightly belonging to their father. Laban can no longer hide his true feelings (*B'reishit* 31:1–2).

45. See comments of Nahum Sarna in *The New JPS Torah Commentary*, Genesis, 212. See also J. Feliks in תחומים 3:461(1982).

God now reveals Himself to Jacob: "Return to the land of your fathers, your birthplace, and I will be with you" (*B'reishit* 31:3). Jacob asks Rachel and Leah to meet him in the field where he tells them how their father had constantly deceived him. He tells them that God's angel had revealed the secret that enabled him to counter Laban's deceptions saying to him, "Train your eyes and see how all of the males that couple with the flocks are streaked and mottled, for I know what Laban has been doing to you." Jacob further tells his wives that God has spoken, saying, "I am the God of Bet-El where you anointed a pillar and where you made a vow to Me. Now, arise and leave this land and return to your native land." This revelation serves to underscore the reliability of the dream Jacob had when he left his father's house many years earlier. With the ready acquiescence of his wives, Jacob readies himself, his family, and his possessions for flight (*B'reishit* 31:13–18).

While Laban is away shearing his sheep, Rachel unaccountably steals Laban's household idols called "*teraphim*" in the Torah. Jacob is unaware of Rachel's act (*B'reishit* 31:18–20). When Laban discovers that Jacob and his family have fled, he follows in hot pursuit and he and his company catch up with them at Mount Gilead in Transjordan. Laban confronts Jacob and with barely concealed anger, says to him, "What have you done? You misled me and took away my daughters like prisoners of war . . . I would have sent you away with celebration, with songs accompanied by timbrel and lyre. You didn't even allow me to kiss my sons and daughters. It was a foolish thing for you to have done" (*B'reishit* 31:26). As he continues, he tells Jacob that Jacob's God had warned him in a dream to do no harm to him, though he certainly has the power to do so. He then angrily asks his son-in-law that if he was so anxious to leave, why then did he, Jacob, steal his gods. But Jacob knows nothing of Rachel's theft. He tells Laban that he left surreptitiously because he feared that Laban would steal Rachel and Leah away from him. Jacob then says, "But anyone with whom you find your gods shall not remain alive" – an ominous statement indeed. Laban then conducts an intrusive search in which finds nothing. This raises Jacob's ire further. Among other matters, Jacob reiterates his years of faithful service under harsh and unforgiving terms and how he was cheated at every turn. Only the God of his fathers assured his ultimate success.

An equally angry Laban retorts that in any case, "The daughters are my daughters, the children and my children, the flocks are my flocks – it's all mine!" (*B'reishit* 31:31–43).

But Laban knows that at this point he cannot prevail, and the two men agree to a pact. Jacob agrees that he will not cross over the marked location of the pact toward Aram-Naharaim and Laban will not cross over to Eretz Yisrael. It is noteworthy that none of Jacob's sons will seek wives from the Aramean branch of the family, as did Isaac and Jacob. From this point on, the people of Jacob are rendered distinct from the other descendants of Terach, Abraham's father. Laban contracts the agreement in the name of his gods, whereas Jacob swears only in the name of the God of Isaac.

But why did Rachel take Laban's household gods? According to one theory suggested by modern scholars based upon archaeological evidence, Rachel was driven by Nuzi law, which said that whoever possesses the household gods is entitled to the birthright.[46] Just as Jacob stole the blessing of the birthright from his father, Rachel, his first love, steals the birthright from her father. But just as Jacob paid a terrible price for his birthright, Rachel will also pay a terrible price. Jacob's assertion that whoever has these objects will not live proves tragically prophetic when a short time later Rachel dies in childbirth to her second son, Benjamin.

Jacob and Laban go their separate ways. Advancing closer to his native land, Jacob is met by a band of angels. When Jacob had his initial great dream many years earlier, he saw ascending and descending angels on a ladder bridging the gap between heaven and earth. Rashi there contended that the ascending angels at that time were the angels of Eretz Yisrael who were leaving Jacob. The descending angels were the angels that would accompany Jacob in the exile. Rashi now says that as Jacob leaves Laban forever, he is being met by the angels of the Land of Israel, who are

46. *The New JPS Torah Commentary*, 216.

greeting him upon his return. Whatever the case, this meeting represents the beginning of a new chapter of his life, marked by renewed and renewing faith. Jacob calls this place Mahanaim, which means "double camp." This seems to confirm one of the messages of Jacob's initial dream: Reality is not one-dimensional and the mundane world of daily experience hides within it another reality containing the angels of God.

Chapter 20

Struggling With Angels and Men

PARASHAT VAYISHLAKH

JACOB, ALWAYS A PRUDENT MAN, sends emissaries to his brother Essau as he approaches his native land. He instructs his men to say, "To my lord Essau, your servant Jacob. Until now I have dwelled with Laban. I have cattle, donkeys, flocks, and male and female slaves, and I am sending this message to tell my lord and to find favor in your eyes" (*B'reishit* 32:5–6). The emissaries return with the ominous news that Essau is coming to meet Jacob with four hundred men. Jacob is filled with trepidation, and as Rashi says, citing a Midrash, he prepares for what may befall him in three ways: giving gifts, offering prayer, and preparing for war (*B'reishit* 32:8–22, Commentary of Rashi on 32:9).

He first divides his camp into two so that if one camp is attacked, the other can flee. He then prays, declaring before God that he is unworthy of the multiple kindnesses already bestowed upon him from above, enriching him and rendering him a father of a large family that is numerous enough to be divided into two camps. He must now implore God to save him from his brother Essau, who could smite him "from mother unto child." He refers back to God's promise to make his seed as abundant as the sand of the sea. With the prayer concluded, Jacob arranges an elaborate display of gifts for Essau, comprising valuable animals divided into separate flocks to be delivered at staged intervals. Each factotum attending the separate flocks is to respond to Essau's expected questions, "From your servant Jacob, a gift for my lord Essau, for Jacob is coming in turn." With this grand display of graciousness, Jacob hopes to appease the brother he fled so many years earlier in fear of his life (*B'reishit* 32:4–21).

When the night descends, Jacob takes his entire family across the Jabbok ford, but he remains alone on the other side. The sages say that he returned to gather up the "small jars" that remained behind (*Hullin* 91a). But then a phantom-being attacks Jacob and they begin to wrestle through the night until the breaking of the dawn (*B'reishit* 32:33–27). This "man" sees that he cannot subdue Jacob. He touches Jacob's thigh at the hip socket and dislocates it as they wrestle. He then turns to Jacob and says, "Let me go, for morning has broken." Jacob refuses and says, "I will not let you go until you bless me."

The most penetrating treatment of this theophany comes to us from Rashi. As Rashi would have it, Jacob is demanding that this being confirm the legitimacy of his appropriation of the blessing of his father Isaac, a blessing that Essau claimed as legitimately his (Commentary on *B'reishit* 32:27).

This being then asks Jacob his name, and Jacob tells him. The "man" then says, "It will no longer be said that your name is Jacob, but rather ישראל – Israel, for you struggle with angels and men and you prevail" (*B'reishit* 32:29).

In Isaac's home, before Jacob fled to Haran, when Essau learned what Jacob had done to him, he said, "How fitting that they named him יעקב – Jacob, וַיַּעְקְבֵנִי זֶה פַעֲמַיִם, for he tricked me, יַעְקְבֵנִי – *ya'akveini* twice, once when he took my birthright and now that he took my blessing" (*B'reishit* 27:36). Rashi explains the underlying meaning of the phantom-being's words to be, "No [longer will your name be] Jacob – they will no longer claim that Isaac's blessings came to you only through trickery and deception, but rather through preeminence and right." Rashi then cites a passage from the later prophet Hosea.

In the womb he supplanted his brother,	בַּבֶּטֶן עָקַב אֶת אָחִיו
In manhood he struggled with a divine being,	וּבְאוֹנוֹ שָׂרָה אֶת אֱ־לֹהִים
He struggled and prevailed over an angel	וַיָּשַׂר אֶל מַלְאָךְ וַיֻּכָל
Who wept and implored him.	בָּכָה וַיִּתְחַנֶּן לוֹ

(Hosea 12:4–5)

The "man," now identified by the prophet as an angel, accedes to Jacob's demand for legitimization by changing his name. Jacob becomes ישראל – Israel. This name is playfully related by the angel to ישר א־ל – *yisar E-l*, he who subdued God's angel (Commentary on *B'reishit* 32:29).

But who is this angel? This is, in fact, Jacob's question. After the angel asks Jacob's name and changes it to Israel, Jacob asks for the angel's name. The angel responds with a question. "Why do you ask my name?" Instead of answering, he blesses Jacob (*B'reishit* 32:30).

In a parallel passage in the Book of Judges, Manoah, the father of Samson, will ask the same question of the angel that appears to him and his wife to foretell Samson's birth. That angel responds with the identical question, "Why do you ask my name?" and then adds, "It is unknowable" (Judge 13:17). The sages tell us that such angels are called into existence solely for a single task. They have no persona and therefore they have no name. In soaring poetic imagery, we are told that each day, angels emerge from a perpetually flowing river of fire, sing their praise to God, and resubmerge into that river (*B'reishit Rabba* 78:1).

Rashi joins that tradition with another, cited in the same textual source, saying that this angel's single task is to serve as the patron angel of Essau (Commentary on *B'reishit* 32:25–27; *B'reishit Rabba* 77:3). Following this line of thought, Jacob's flesh-and-blood confrontation with Essau is preceded by his confrontation with the being that represents what Essau is about, and Jacob defeats him.

But victory comes at a price. The angel has wounded his thigh, and in the morning, Jacob is left limping (*B'reishit* 32:26,32).

Let us consider the character of this wound. When Abraham instructed his servant to "put his hand under my thigh" and swear that he would find only the appropriate wife for Isaac, Jacob's father, the term "thigh" is, as we explained, almost certainly a euphemism for Abraham's organ of generation. Further, one biblical idiom frequently used for descent from a male is "those who issue from his thigh." Certainly here, the context is clear that in Jacob's case, "thigh" is literally intended. Presumably, Essau's patron angel really would want to attack

Jacob's posterity, and the attack on Jacob's thigh is an act of psychological displacement in which the angel's intent is the destruction of Jacob's procreative power. The attack on the nerves in Jacob's thigh is a euphemism in action, a point obliquely hinted by Ibn Ezra (Commentary on *B'reishit* 32:33). Thus, Ramban cites a Midrash to the effect that this angel will continue to strike "at all the righteous who will emerge from [Jacob]" (Commentary on *B'reishit* 32:36). He goes on to say that the entire theophany alludes to the descendants of Jacob. They will be condemned to struggle against adversaries symbolized by Essau and his angel who seek to destroy Israel root and branch. (Ramban and *Vayikra Rabba* 11).

Since this experience leaves Jacob limping, the Torah says, "Therefore the children of Israel refrain from eating the sciatic nerve from the hip joint to this very day" (*B'reishit* 32:33). This is a reference to the Halakhic rule that the entire nerve and each channel from it must be carefully removed before one can contemplate eating the hinds of a kosher animal (*Hullin* 92b).

Now according to the upshot of the Talmudic dialectical discussion, nerves and sinews have no desirable taste and, by Halakhic rule, normally do not fall under the rubric of forbidden food. But as a consequence of Jacob's struggle, the Torah assigns this nerve a negative significance (*Hullin* 92b, 99–100; Tosefta 7:2). Its removal before consumption commemorates and canonizes this theophany. Jacob's struggle is thus elevated to a paradigm for Israel's claim to the birthright and the legacy of Abraham and Isaac. But this legacy cannot be taken for granted. Israel must struggle with angels and men, with both matter and spirit forever, and then become worthy of the birthright.

Furthermore, this birthright is a disputed birthright. While Essau's patron angel has conceded the point, it is not clear that the Essau of flesh and blood will. The question of legitimacy will continue to dog Jacob. At Beth-E-l, God Himself will have to tell Jacob again, "Your name is Jacob. You will no longer be called Jacob, but Israel shall be your name." And, "indeed, he called his name Israel" (*B'reishit* 35:10). But in the continuing narrative of the Torah, both the names of Jacob and Israel will be used apparently interchangeably. The sages comment that the name Jacob is not uprooted, but rather Israel becomes primary and Jacob is secondary (*B'rakhot* 13a). Ramban argues that when Jacob is used, it is used to tell us that Jacob is subservient, and when Israel is used, he is preeminent (Commentary on *B'reishit* 42:2).

The anxiety over legitimacy will continue to hover over Jacob even on his deathbed. Toward the end of *B'reishit*, Jacob's son Joseph, a younger son made preeminent over Jacob's firstborn Reuben, will bring his own sons Manasseh and Ephraim to be blessed. Like Isaac before him, Jacob's eyes are now dim. To help his father, Joseph will place his firstborn, Manasseh, at Jacob's right hand and his younger son, Ephraim, at his left. Jacob crisscrosses his hands, placing his right hand on the younger Ephraim and his left on Manasseh. Joseph assumes that Jacob has simply been mistaken because of his blindness and will attempt to switch Jacob's hand back, saying "That is not right father. The other is the firstborn; place your right hand on his head." Jacob refuses saying, "I know, son, I know. He too will become a people and he too will be great, but his younger brother will be even greater; his descendants will be the fullness of nations" (*B'reishit* 48:8–20).

The concern of the legitimacy about the birthright will not even end with Jacob's death. When Moses will be sent back to Pharaoh in Egypt to demand Israel's freedom, God will say, "Israel is my firstborn son" (*Sh'mot* 4:22). Rashi then comments, "It is here that God signs on to the sale of the birthright that Jacob purchased from Essau" (Commentary ad locum).

If we follow the Midrashic traditions cited by Ramban (32:26), the struggle for legitimization is an ongoing historical struggle. How else are we to understand it when both the Christian and Moslem powers of later history insist that Israel was "rejected by God" and that the "real" Israel is Christianity or Islam, respectively? How else shall we construe the attempt on both the hard Right and the hard Left to reduce the modern State of Israel into a pariah, illegitimate state?

But to return to our narrative, the Torah makes the point that this theophany transforms Jacob. He calls this site P'niel, face of God – "For I have seen divinity face to face and my life has been preserved" (*B'reishit* 32:31).

When the sages say that Jacob returned across the Jabbok ford to retrieve "small jugs," we can complete the thought and understand it to mean that Jacob returned to look for things of little worth and found his destiny instead (*Hullin* 91a).

Having struggled with Essau's angelic patron through the night, Jacob now prepares to meet the Essau of flesh and blood. He divides his wives and children into discrete units to be introduced to his brother. In great deference, he bows to the ground before his brother seven times. Essau runs up to greet him, embracing him, falling on his neck, kissing him, and both brothers weep (*B'reishit* 33:1–5). Jacob will tell his brother, "Seeing your face is like seeing the face of divinity." But this is ironic because Essau, presumably, knows nothing of the great theophany that preceded the meeting (*B'reishit* 33:10).

How are we to take the great warmth displayed here in a meeting that Jacob approached with such trepidation? In *B'reishit Rabba* we are presented with the following. Rabbi Yannai looks at this with a jaundiced eye (*B'reishit Rabba* 78:9). In his view it is nothing but an elaborate hypocritical display of false emotion. With broad humor, he says that when Essau fell on Jacob's neck, he intended to bite him. Miraculously, Jacob's neck turned to marble. Essau wept because he broke his teeth, and Jacob wept because it hurt.

However, Rashi cites a different view, and he quotes a different Midrash (*Sifrei Bahalotkha* 69). There, Rabbi Simeon bar Yohai says, "It is a well-founded principle that Essau hates Jacob. But at this point, compassion overcame him and he embraced his brother with all his heart" (Commentary on *B'reishit* 33:4). This construction suggests hopefulness and it adds nuance to our understanding of the great fratricidal rivalry.

When Isaac dies, Jacob and Essau will join together as brothers to bury their father (*B'reishit* 35:29). At the end, let there be hope.

Chapter 21

Rape, Revenge, and Redemption

PARASHAT VAYISHLAKH

After the departure of Essau, Jacob proceeds first to Succot in Transjordan and then to Shechem in the Promised Land. For the second time, the Torah records a patriarchal purchase of real estate in the land (*B'reishit* 33:18–20). Abraham had purchased the gravesite of Machpelah in Hebron as a perpetual heritage site for the people that would emerge from his loins. Jacob now purchases a field at Shechem and builds an altar to E-l, E-lohai Yisrael.

But tragedy will soon follow. Dinah, Leah's daughter, setting out to visit with the young girls of the land, is seized and raped by Shechem son of Hamor, a prince of the land. The rapist, who does not allow Dinah to return home, decides that he is in love with his victim and seeks to appeal to her heart. At the same time he convinces his father to enter into negotiations with Jacob for her hand in marriage (*B'reishit* 34:1–4).

Jacob is stunned by the news of his daughter's defilement and captivity, but he remains silent until Dinah's brothers arrive home. They are understandably furious (*B'reishit* 34:5–7). The Torah frames their state of mind with the words:

> כִּי נְבָלָה עָשָׂה בְיִשְׂרָאֵל לִשְׁכַּב אֶת בַּת יַעֲקֹב וְכֵן לֹא יֵעָשֶׂה
>
> For he had committed an outrage in Israel by lying with a daughter of Jacob – a thing not to be done!

In fact, as Rashi comments, this act of kidnap and rape was not only an outrage in Israel, but a violation of universally acknowledged norms (Commentary on verse 7).

Now Shechem, accompanied by his father Hamor, contacts Jacob and the family, and Hamor puts forward a far-reaching proposal. "Let us marry with each other. We will offer our young women to you in marriage and we will marry your daughters. You can live with us and the land will be open to you. Settle, move about (or, according to Radak and Seforno 34:10, 'do business') and acquire holdings here" (*B'reishit* 34:9–10).

Now the fine prospective groom, Shechem, speaks. He promises to pay any bride price that is demanded for Dinah's hand (*B'reishit* 34:11–12). As Professor Nahum Sarna notes, the proposal is intrinsically insulting, reducing the issue at hand to mere monetary consideration.[47]

We should note that Dinah is still being held as a captive by Shechem. As Radak notes, while Jacob remains silent, it is the sons who respond, and they have no compunctions about being entirely deceptive as they deal with the rapist and his father (*B'reishit* 34:13 and commentary of Radak). They respond that under no circumstances can their sister be allowed to marry an uncircumcised man whose foreskin is disgusting and an affront to them (*B'reishit* 34:13–15 and commentary of Rashi). However, if the inhabitants of Shechem all agree to be circumcised, they will accept Hamor's far-reaching proposal and the Israelites and the Shechemites will unite as one people (*B'reishit* 34:15–17).

Shechem attends to the matter forthwith, and father and son begin to promote the proposal among their own people. As the commentators note, when Hamor presents the proposal to his people, he is careful to reverse the order of benefits. When he spoke to Jacob, he said that the Shechemites would first give their daughters to the Israelites as wives and then take Israelite women. Speaking to his own people, he reverses the order. "We will take their daughters as wives and will (then) give them our daughters" (*B'reishit* 34:21). He further sweetens the proposal promising that the Shechemites will be able to appropriate Israel's wealth (*B'reishit* 34:24).

47. JPS commentary, ad locum.

The Shechemites willingly agree and engage in a mass circumcision. On the third day, when they remain immobilized by pain, Simeon and Levi, two of the full brothers of Dinah, enter the town armed, kill the entire male population including Shechem and Hamor, and rescue their sister. The other brothers strip the corpses, despoil the town, and take the women and children captive (*B'reishit* 34:25–29).

When Jacob hears what his sons have done, he is horrified. Turning to Simeon and Levi, he says, "You have muddied the waters for me, making me odious among the inhabitants of the land" (*B'reishit* 34:30). He protests that the Israelites are a tiny minority, and if the inhabitants of the land decide to take action, the Israelites could be totally destroyed. But the brothers are adamant. "Shall our sister be treated as a whore?"

What are we to make of this exchange? Apparently, Jacob is only asserting that Simeon and Levi's destruction of the male population was dangerously imprudent. But is prudence all that is at stake here? What moral judgment is the Torah rendering upon Simeon and Levi?

Here we must enter upon a dispute in interpretation between Rambam and Ramban. For Rambam, Simeon and Levi only delivered deserved punishment to the Shechemites. According to the Halakha, all descendants of Noah – the whole human race – are obligated to observe seven prohibitions. Universally prohibited are: idolatry, cursing God's name, murder, incest and adultery, theft, eating the flesh of a living animal, and violating "civil norms" or what the Rabbis call דינים – *dinim* (*Mishneh Torah, Hilkhot Melakhim* 9:1). As Rambam understands the full implication of "civil norms," all human societies are obligated to establish courts of law that will punish anti-social behavior. The Shechemites not only did not do this, but acquiesced in the rape and seizure of Dinah. Therefore, the Shechemites were all guilty of a capital offense in not enforcing *dinim* (*Hilkhot Melakhim* 9:14 cf. *Sanhedrin* 56b).

However, Ramban strongly dissents from Rambam on this point. It is certainly true that there is a universal obligation to establish courts of justice, but failure to do so does not condemn each Noahide to death. Nor is it clear that Jacob's sons had either the right or duty to serve a judge, witness, and executioner. Later, in the time of Moses, the multiple sins of the Canaanites will serve as the warrant for Israelite conquest – but that is later.

Jacob was silent when Dinah's brothers deceptively agreed to the union with the Shechemites, while inducing the Shechemites to engage in mass circumcision. That scheme would allow the rescue of Dinah and perhaps the death of Shechem and Hamor, her captors. But that is a far cry from wiping out the entire male population. Jacob's initial reaction was to protest the rashness and dangerous risks involved in the brothers' actions threatening the lives of the entire family. But in no way does this exhaust Jacob's concerns.

Later, upon his deathbed, Jacob speaks to the future destiny of the descendants of each of his sons. To Simeon and Levi he says,

Simeon and Levi are brothers,	שִׁמְעוֹן וְלֵוִי אַחִים
Their wares are the tools of violence.	כְּלֵי חָמָס מְכֵרֹתֵיהֶם
Let not my person join their council,	בְּסֹדָם אַל תָּבֹא נַפְשִׁי
Let not my being be part of their community.	בִּקְהָלָם אַל תֵּחַד כְּבֹדִי
For in their anger they killed men,	כִּי בְאַפָּם הָרְגוּ אִישׁ
In their willfulness they tore down walls.[48]	וּבִרְצֹנָם עִקְּרוּ שׁוֹר
Cursed be their anger so fierce,	אָרוּר אַפָּם כִּי עָז
their fury so relentless.	וְעֶבְרָתָם כִּי קָשָׁתָה
I will divide them in Jacob,	אֲחַלְּקֵם בְּיַעֲקֹב
Spread them through Israel. (*B'reishit* 49:5–7)	וַאֲפִיצֵם בְּיִשְׂרָאֵל

Here Jacob is denouncing the immorality of their acts and not merely the rashness of it all. In radical contrast to Rambam's judgment, for Ramban, Jacob's final denunciation serves as the Torah's last word on the actions of the brothers. However, in the aftermath of Simeon and Levi's deeds, the immediate threats to his family had to be Jacob's concern.

After this episode, God commands Jacob to return to Beth E-l, the place where he had first fled from his brother Essau so many years earlier. As he travels from Shechem, the Torah tells us, the "terror of God" pervaded the towns and the inhabitants

48. I am following Ibn Ezra in translating this phrase. See his comments ad locum.

did not pursue Jacob's sons (*B'reishit* 35:6). Much later, Jacob will assign Shechem as an allotment to the descendants of Joseph, "which I acquired with my bow and my sword" (*B'reishit* 48:22). A Midrashic tradition assumes that this means that Jacob initially had to take defensive action against potential Canaanite avengers (Rashi on 48:22, *Midrash Vayisau* in JD Eisenstein, *Otsar HaMidrashim*, 157).

Let us now focus upon the journey to Beth E-l. Jacob now orders his family to remove all fetishes of alien gods from their midst. Jacob takes all the idolatrous materials and earrings surrendered by his sons and buries them under an oak tree near Shechem (*B'reishit* 35:4). Presumably, these items were all part of the spoils of Shechem (Rashi and Radak, ad locum). Further, Jacob instructs his children to purify themselves and change their clothes as they ready themselves for their father's return to Beth E-l. There, Jacob had dreamed about a ladder with ascending and descending angels connecting God and man. There he had vowed that Y-H-V-H would be his God.

The return to Beth E-l could not be tainted by the idols of Shechem. In that place God will confirm Jacob's assumption of the name Israel and his succession to the covenant of Abraham and Isaac.

Chapter 22

Joseph and His Brothers, Part I: Vanity, Fratricidal Hatred, and Personal Growth

PARASHAT VAYESHEV

RACHEL, THE LOVE OF JACOB'S LIFE, dies in childbirth on the journey to Hebron, bequeathing to him Joseph and Benjamin (*B'reishit* 35:16–20). The story of Joseph is well known, but let us review the salient points. Joseph, Rachel's eldest son, is showered with Jacob's undisguised special favor, arousing the jealousy of his brothers and continuing the rivalry of Rachel and Leah into the next generation. Especially galling is the special cloak that Jacob confers upon Joseph in his seventeenth year. Joseph exacerbates the angry hatred of Leah's children by consorting specifically with the children of the two handmaidens, Zilpah and Bilhah, and then bringing back tales to their father (*B'reishit* 36:1–4).

Matters become far worse when Joseph announces his vainglorious dreams. In his first dream, he and his brothers are binding sheaves in the field. Joseph's sheaf stands erect, while his brothers' sheaves bow down to his sheaf. In his second dream, in an incredibly presumptuous projection, the sun, moon, and eleven stars bow down to him. This is too much even for his adoring father who becomes angry, saying to him, "Am I, your mother, and your brothers supposed to bow down to you?" But while his brothers' jealous rage grows more toxic, "his father kept the matter in mind" (*B'reishit* 37:5–11).

The sages portray the young Joseph as vain and utterly self-focused, curling his locks and using his eyes to draw attention to himself (*B'reishit Rabba* 84:7). At this stage, Joseph becomes the negative paradigm for the dangerously spoiled child, and the sages use his story as the precautionary tale warning against favoring one child over the others. For the sake of the gift of a more expensive cloak "his brothers envied him and events were set into motion that led to our ancestors' descent into Egypt (and Egyptian slavery)" (*Shabbat* 10b).

Jacob sends Joseph to Shechem to report on his brothers who are there tending flocks. He sets out from "the valley of Hebron," where his father is staying, to Shechem in the north (*B'reishit* 37:12–14). It is noteworthy that Hebron will ultimately be the patrimony of the tribe of Judah and it will be Judah who will play a key role in selling Joseph into slavery. Shechem, the place of Joseph's undoing, will later belong to the tribes of Joseph.

When Joseph comes into view of his brothers, one of them derisively announces, "Here comes the dreamer." They plot against him. "Then, let us kill him and cast his corpse into a pit. We can say that a wild animal ate him and we will then see what will become of his dreams" (*B'reishit* 37:19–20).

There can be no doubt of their serious intent. Reuben, the eldest brother and presumably the most levelheaded at this point in time, is sufficiently alarmed to offer a plan of his own to buy time and enable him to save Joseph. Playing along with his brothers, Reuben cautions them against shedding his blood outright, but suggests they simply lower him into a pit and abandon him there, for this will allow Reuben to come back later and rescue his brother (*B'reishit* 37:21–22).

Now Reuben has his own history of family rivalry and anger. In his youth he had been witness to his mother Leah's humiliation at the hands of Rachel, who could successfully vie for Jacob's sexual attention (*B'reishit* 30:14–16). When Rachel dies, Reuben, inflamed by his mother's humiliation, rapes Rachel's handmaiden, Bilhah, mother of two of Jacob's children, presumably to set her sexually out of bounds to Jacob (*B'reishit* 37:19–22 cf. *Shabbat* 55b).[49] But that horrific act occurred when Reuben

49. Well known is the Aggadic statement that says, "He who says Reuben sinned is in error." (See also Rashi to *B'reishit* 37:19–22) Rather, Reuben merely 'disarranged' Jacob's bed. But the surest way to 'disarrange' someone's bed is to sleep

was much younger. The sages imagine Reuben as the ultimate penitent, wearing sackcloth and constantly fasting in penance for his violation of Bilhah (Rashi commentary on *B'reishit* 37:29 cf. *B'reishit Rabba* 82:11). It is therefore unthinkable for him to stand by while another family outrage is perpetrated. His advice is taken. The brothers strip Joseph of his hated special cloak and lower him into a pit.

Now Reuben temporarily absents himself while the brothers sit down to eat. As they sit there, they witness an Ishmaelite caravan coming in their direction, loaded with goods for sale in Egypt. Judah now has a suggestion about what can be done with Joseph. He says, "What profit is there in killing our brother and covering his blood? Let us sell him to the Ishmaelites instead of physically murdering him – he is after all our flesh [and blood]" (*B'reishit* 37:28–29). The brothers readily agree. Meanwhile, another caravan, this time a Midianite caravan, passes by. However, we now confront an ambiguity in the text. The Torah says, "Midianite merchants pass by and draw Joseph out of the pit and sell him to the Ishmaelites for twenty pieces of silver; then they take Joseph down to Egypt" (*B'reishit* 37:28).

But who exactly is selling Joseph to the Ishmaelites? Is it the brothers or is it the Midianites? Rashbam champions the view that while the brothers were discussing the merits of selling their brother, it was the Midianite merchants who actually saw Joseph in the pit, drew him up, and sold him to the Ishmaelites (Comments on *B'reishit* 37:28). It is important to recognize that Rashbam is not trying to exonerate the brothers. If Rashbam is correct in his reading of the text, in some ways their passivity actually makes them more contemptible.

Reuben now returns and finds the pit empty. In grief and

---

with his wife. One should first note the Mishna: Megillah 25a: "The act of Reuben must be read (as part of the weekly Torah reading) but should not be publicly translated." This prohibition only makes sense if the Torah is saying that Reuben had relations with Bilhah. The above quoted Aggada should be understood as a plea for respectful euphemistic treatment of the father of a tribe of Israel. Literalism is not called for here and taking this Aggada literally makes the sages sound like children, which they most assuredly were not.

horror, he tears his clothes and exclaims to his brothers "The boy isn't there. Where am I now supposed to go?" (*B'reishit* 37:29–30).

The sobering realization descends upon the brothers that they must now face their father and tell him that Joseph is gone. They slaughter a goat, dip Joseph's cloak into its blood, and bring it back to their father with the words: "We found this. Tell us whether this belongs to your son or not" (*B'reishit* 37:32–33). Jacob tears his clothes as he recognizes the bloody cloak and concludes that a wild animal killed Joseph. He descends into deep depression and none of his children can relieve him. Joseph's disappearance will not only haunt Jacob, but the entire family will descend into gloom with him (*B'reishit* 37:34–35). Meanwhile, Joseph has been taken down to Egypt where he is bought as a slave by Potiphar, chief courtier of the Pharaoh (*B'reishit* 37:36).

At this point, the text diverts from Joseph's story and recounts events in the life of Judah. But let us now continue with the Joseph story. Although Joseph is now Potiphar's slave, God's favor remains with Joseph even under those circumstances, and whatever he does prospers. Recognizing Joseph's special talents, Potiphar promotes him to the point that "he left all that he had in Joseph's hands and (with him there) he paid attention to nothing save the food that he ate" (*B'reishit* 39:6).

Now the Torah notes that Joseph was well built and handsome and Potiphar's wife becomes sexually obsessed by him. She tries to seduce him. But with whatever inner hesitations, Joseph refuses her advances and couches his protestation in moral terms. "My master is paying no attention to my activities at home, placing all matters into my hands. No one is superior to me in this household and he denies me nothing apart from you, his wife. How could I do such a wicked thing and sin before God?" (*B'reishit* 39:8–9). But the woman persists in her demands. One day when no one else is around, she seizes him by his cloak and demands, "Make love to me!" Joseph flees her advances, leaving his cloak in her hands. The now furious woman cries out to the household servants exclaiming, "Look! He brought in a Hebrew man to mock us. He came on to me seeking to have intercourse with me, so I cried out loudly. When he heard me raising my voice and crying out, he left his cloak in my hands and fled." Potiphar returns home, hears his wife's story and has Joseph imprisoned (*B'reishit* 39:10–20).

Joseph, in the fullness of youthful vigor, resists temptation out of a decent regard for his master's trust and out of reverence for God, and pays a terrible price. We are no longer dealing with a vainglorious, spoiled child, but a young man with moral principles and the discipline to live by them.

The masters of the Masoretic text of the Torah, who provided us with the cantillation point on the words of the text, mark the word וימאן – "he refused" [her advances] – with a *shalshelet*, which directs an extended and hesitant singing of the word, effectively positing a wrenching inner struggle for Joseph. Resisting great temptation is never easy, and the sages speculate about the inner resources that were decisive for him. One rendering, cited by Rashi, suggests that at that moment, Joseph imagined his father peering through the window rebuking him. This fortified his determination not to betray the values he learned in his father's house (Rashi on *B'reishit* 39:11; *Sotah* 36b). It is this moment more than any other that moved Jewish tradition to refer to Joseph as יוסף הצדיק, "Joseph the saint," and the שומר הברית, "the guardian of the covenant" (Talmud *Yoma* 35b, *Zohar* I 59). By refusing to misuse his sexuality in an adulterous act with Potiphar's wife, he guarded the sanctity of the covenant of circumcision that consecrates the sexuality of the male Israelite to the God of Abraham and the values that God demands of his servants.

This narrative prepares us for the further transformations in Joseph's character.

Chapter 23

Joseph and His Brothers, Part II: The Temptation of Judah

PARASHAT VAYESHEV

In advance of the narrative of Joseph in Potiphar's house, the Torah digresses, telling us the story of Judah and a very different account of sexual temptation. Judah marries and has three sons: Er, Onan, and Shelah. When Er comes of age, Judah arranges a marriage for him with a woman named Tamar. But the Torah tells us, "Er was wicked in God's eyes and God brings about his death" (*B'reishit* 38:1–7). Ramban maintains that this statement about Er's death forewarns us not to conclude that this is punishment for Judah's sinful dealings with Joseph. Rather, we are to focus upon what is about to occur with fresh attention upon the unfolding story (Commentary on *B'reishit* 38:7).

Judah now instructs his second son, Onan, to take Tamar as a wife in place of Er in order to have children on Er's behalf. In explicit terms, Judah tells Onan to enact *yibum* with her (*B'reishit* 38:8). This foreshadows a commandment that will be legislated in *Sefer Devarim* (*Devarim* 25:5–10). When a man dies without offspring, his brother has a *prima facia* obligation to take his sister-in-law as a wife to bring children into the world in place of the deceased brother and on his behalf.

It is important to note that under all other circumstances, the Torah rules that one's sister-in-law is forbidden. To take her as a wife is a violation of the incest code and would constitute a mortal sin (*Vayikra* 20:21). But in the interest of bringing forth children in place of the lost procreative potential of the deceased, the Torah sets the incest prohibition aside. As Ramban notes, the Book of Ruth testifies to an extended practice of *yibum* in ancient Israel even by relatives more distant than a surviving brother. In that narrative, Boaz, in marrying Ruth, widow of a more distant relative Mahlon, is performing the practice of *yibum* even though the Torah does not obligate him to do so. The Book of Ruth is a story written in praise of loving-kindness (Midrash *Ruth Rabba* 2:15). Boaz and Ruth's willingness to practice *yibum* represents "kindness to the living and the dead" – kindness to Naomi, the bereaved mother, to Ruth, the bereaved wife, and to Mahlon, the deceased and childless husband of Ruth (Ruth 2:20). So meritorious is this act of kindness that from Boaz and Ruth's union, the royal house of David will emerge (Ruth 4:18–21; Commentary of Ramban on *B'reishit* 38:8–10).

But to return to our story, Onan has no interest in bringing forth children on behalf of Er, though he is perfectly willing to enjoy the sexual pleasure proffered by Tamar. When he would have relations with her he would ejaculate outside her body, "spilling his seed upon the ground so as not to provide offspring for his brother." His selfishness is punished by his demise (*B'reishit* 38:9–10).

Now Shelah, brother to Er and Onan, remains, and he could also be called upon to engage in *yibum*. Judah now equivocates telling Tamar to remain a widow until "Shelah is old enough," but the day does not arrive; Judah fears that Shelah might also die in a marriage to Tamar (*B'reishit* 38:11).

Years pass and Judah's own wife dies. Subsequently, Judah is at a sheep shearing celebration at Timnah, and Tamar hears about this. She removes her widow garments that she has been wearing all this time and she disguises herself as a cult prostitute, but veils her face and awaits Judah at a crossroad. Judah sees her without recognizing her. Now Judah has been bereft of a wife and when he sees Tamar, he approaches her, offering to send a young goat in payment for her services. She demands and receives his seal, cord, and staff as collateral until the goat is sent. When Judah leaves her, she returns home and puts on her widow garments once again. Judah, an honest man, sends the kid in payment for the prostitute's services, but no one in the area knows anything about this cult prostitute he wants to pay. Embarrassed by the entire affair, Judah abandons all thought of recovering the collateral (*B'reishit* 38:12–23).

About three months later, word reaches him that Tamar is pregnant. Judah is outraged by this impropriety and demands that Tamar be burned to death (*B'reishit* 38:24). The extreme character of the penalty he demands is without precedent in the Torah's legislation regarding the widow awaiting *yibum*, so Ramban speculates that perhaps Judah's status in Canaan gave him the power to exact any penalty for a personal affront (Commentary on *B'reishit* 38:21–22).

But Tamar is not a passive victim. She sends Judah the seal, cord, and staff she had taken as collateral with the words, "I am with child by the man to whom these belong." And she adds, "Examine these. Whose seal, cord, and staff are these?" This is, of course, an embarrassing moment of truth for Judah, but he owns up to his responsibility. He says, "She is more decent than I. She did this because I did not allow her to marry my son, Shelah" (*B'reishit* 38:25–26).

The Midrash comments that when Judah saw Tamar disguised as a prostitute, he was about to pass her by, but "the angel in charge of lust" forced him to engage her sexually (*B'reishit Rabba* 85:8). Apart from the obvious humor in saying, "The angel made him do it," there is a profounder analysis at work here. While Judah's motivation at that moment is self-evident, Tamar's motivation requires some thought. In disguising herself as a prostitute and seducing Judah, she was clearly debasing herself and, as we have seen, putting herself in great danger. But so important to her was the duty of *yibum*, bringing children into the world on behalf of her late husband, that she was prepared to do all of it. By contrast to Judah, her motivations are "for the sake of heaven." In the tension and interplay of the motivations of these two people, Judah's male sexual needs become, in effect, Tamar's angel that brings about *yibum* and ultimately will produce kings in Israel.

It is important to take note that once the Torah is given, not even *yibum* will be allowed to set aside the incest prohibition against a father-in-law having sexual relations with his daughter-in-law

(*Vayikra* 20:12). But the events involving Judah and Tamar occur before the Torah's stricter incest code is enacted. In rabbinic terms, Judah and Tamar were bound by the more lenient incest regulations of the Children of Noah (Rambam, *Hilkhot Melakhim* 9:5). So important to Tamar was her obligation to her dead husband that she was prepared to have relations with a father-in-law for whom she almost certainly had no sexual feelings.

Let us now re-examine one element in the previous Joseph story. Judah and his brothers, as part of their concealment of their role in Joseph's disappearance, take his cloak and dip it in the blood of a goat to convince their father, Jacob, that Joseph was killed by a wild animal. They present the bloody cloak to Jacob saying, "Examine it. Is this your son's cloak or not?" (*B'reishit* 37:32). Now, at Judah's moment of truth when he is shown his seal, cord, and staff, Tamar says, "Examine these. To whom belong the seal, cord, and staff?" (*B'reishit* 38:25). Tamar uses the same terms that Judah used to deceive his father and break his heart. To say the least, Judah behaved irresponsibly toward both Joseph and Jacob. Jacob deceived his father, and in return he is deceived by his sons. Judah deceives his father and is deceived in turn by his daughter-in-law Tamar. Tamar's actions compel Judah to own up to a far less grievous act of irresponsibility on his part in relation to her. This entire episode allows us to glimpse Judah's personal growth from the time of his betrayal of his brother. The Torah caps these events by telling us that Judah will never again engage Tamar sexually (*B'reishit* 38:26).

Tamar gives birth to twins, in some ways mirroring the story of the birth of Essau and Jacob. Again, there is ambiguity about which child is her firstborn. At childbirth, an infant's hand emerges, and thc midwife ties red wool on it, exclaiming, "This child came first." But the hand is withdrawn and the second of the twins bursts forth. This infant is named Peretz, which means "bursting forth." The second infant with red wool tied on its hand is called Zerah, or "shining," after the shining red wool. Both children will be the progenitors of important families in the tribe of Judah. But it will be Peretz, who bursts forth beyond his brother's hand, who will be the ancestor of King David. This child of *yibum* will begin the line out of which will come Boaz, who engaged in *yibum* with Ruth. Ruth herself is a Moabite, which means that she is descended from an incestuous relationship between Lot and his daughter. David then will emerge not only from two instances of *yibum*, but also from the incestuous ancestry of Ruth. When the story of Judah and Tamar is read together with the Book of Ruth, the importance of *yibum*, the selfless kindness it represents, and the remarkable possibilities it allows, become all the more underscored.

Just as the story of his sexual temptation allows Joseph to reveal how he has grown from a self-focused, spoiled child into a disciplined moral adult, so too, the story of the sexual temptation of Judah reveals his transformation into responsible adulthood. The juxtaposition of these two narratives prepares for all that is yet to follow in Sefer *B'reishit*.

Chapter 24

Joseph and His Brothers, Part III: The Irony – Dreams and Their Fulfillment

PARASHAT MIKETZ

When Jacob fled from his brother Essau and spent the first night alone at Beth-El, he had a single dream. In that dream, he saw a ladder bridging the abyss dividing heaven and earth. Angels were ascending and descending upon it and God was nearby. By contrast, Joseph has not one, but two dreams. His first dream is located upon the earth, and his second dream occurs in the heavens, but God is not present in either. These are dreams of personal ascendency and glory, disconnected from God, His angels, and the covenant of Abraham.

As previously noted, Joseph reports his dreams to his already alienated brothers and they are met with such furious enmity that, when given the opportunity, they strip Joseph naked, cast him into a pit, and then decide to sell him into slavery. With venom, they derisively exclaim, "We shall see what will become of his dreams!"

In Egypt, as a slave in Potiphar's household, the Torah tells us "God was with him," and Joseph is so successful that his master puts him in charge of his household. In other words, Joseph's dreams of ascendency are fulfilled in the entirely ironic sense that he becomes the ascendant slave.

When Joseph resists the seductions of Potiphar's wife, and she falsely accuses him of attempting to rape her, he is cast down ingloriously and imprisoned. Here too, his dreams are ironically fulfilled. "God is with Joseph" and he becomes the ascendant prisoner (*B'reishit* 39:21–23).

In the course of time, Pharaoh's butler and baker are both imprisoned with him and Joseph befriends them. One morning, Joseph notices their despondency, and when he inquires about what is troubling them, they confide in him. They have both had disturbing dreams and they have no one to interpret those dreams (*B'reishit* 40:1–7). Joseph encourages them to share their dreams with him, and in a striking phrase he says:

> הֲלוֹא לֵא־לֹהִים פִּתְרֹנִים סַפְּרוּ נָא לִי
> Surely the solutions belong to God. Tell them to me. (*B'reishit* 40:8)

The butler first shares his dream and Joseph deciphers its meaning. "In three days, Pharaoh will raise up your head and restore you to your former station. You will place Pharaoh's cup into his hand in the original manner in which you would provide his drink" (*B'reishit* 40:13). Joseph seizes the opportunity, telling the butler his story and asking the butler to present his case before Pharaoh (*B'reishit* 40:14–15).

Encouraged by this happy prediction, the baker relates his dream. Joseph deciphers his dream to mean that in three days, Pharaoh will raise his head from his body and have him impaled. Both predictions prove to be literally accurate, but the butler chooses not to remember Joseph.

Joseph continues to languish in prison for another two years (*B'reishit* 40:16–23; 41:1). He relies upon the butler's intercession, but as he himself has said, "Surely solutions belong to God" and not to man (See commentary of Rashi on *B'reishit* 40:23). Toward the beginning of the Joseph narrative, Ramban aptly describes the overarching theme of the story with the Hebrew proverb:

> הגזרה אמת והחריצות שקר
> The [Divine] decree is true; [human] design is a lie. (Commentary on *B'reishit* 37:15)

The butler is initially of no help at all.

But everything changes when Pharaoh himself experiences a couplet of troubling dreams and no one can satisfactorily explain them. At last, the butler recalls his time in prison together with the baker. "We had with us a Hebrew youth, slave of the chief courtier. We told him [our dreams] and he explained each dream. As he interpreted them, so did it occur. [Pharaoh] restored me to my office and had the other impaled" (*B'reishit* 41:1–13).

Pharaoh now calls for Joseph, who is taken from prison, properly attired, and presented to him. Pharaoh addresses him saying, "I have heard about you, that you have the ability to decipher dreams" (*B'reishit* 41:14–15). But Joseph demurs, "I have no such power. God can respond to Pharaoh's needs" (*B'reishit* 41:16).

Joseph listens to the dreams and responds that Pharaoh's two dreams have a single, urgent message that God is setting before him. There are soon to be seven years of plenty, followed by seven years of famine whose brutal force will swallow up the memory of the bounty that preceded. The slave advises the king to designate a competent and savvy administrator to organize a system of food storage during the years of plenty (*B'reishit* 41:17–36).

Pharaoh now takes counsel with his ministers and Joseph himself is so designated, with powers second only to the king himself. Joseph's own dreams receive new meaning as he ascends to genuine glory. Pharaoh gives Joseph his signet ring and has him girded in linen garments with a gold chain around his neck. He is to ride in the second chariot behind Pharaoh, and wherever he goes, people are commanded to kneel. Joseph's name is changed to *Tsafnat Paneakh,* which Rashbam, Ibn Ezra, and Radak correctly presume to be an Egyptian name (Commentary on *B'reishit* 41:44–45). Egyptologists variously explain this name to mean either "God speaks, He lives" or "Sustainer of Life" (JPS Commentary on *B'reishit* 41:45). Joseph marries a woman who is not only Egyptian, but the daughter of the Priest of On, High Priest of the sun god, Ra (JPS Commentary, ad locum). This Hebrew slave has now enjoyed a mercurial transformation and rises to Egyptian nobility. Joseph has truly arrived (*B'reishit* 41:41–47).

The *Zohar* describes Joseph's situation to this point as "the place of forgetfulness" (*Zohar* I 193). When Joseph's first child is born, he names him מנשה – Menasseh, כִּי נַשַּׁנִי אֱ־לֹהִים אֶת כָּל עֲמָלִי וְאֵת כָּל בֵּית אָבִי, which Rav Sa'adia Gaon explains as "God enabled me to forget all the suffering I endured in my father's house" (Commentary on *B'reishit* 41:51).

Ramban famously raises the moral question: How could Joseph allow his father to remain in a state of anguished ignorance about whether he was alive or dead once he had the power to tell Jacob where he was? Ramban's own answer is that Joseph was waiting to design the conditions that would allow his initial dreams to be completely fulfilled (Commentary on *B'reishit* 42:9). But one could argue that this only compounds Joseph's sin against his father. After all, Ramban himself characterizes the theme of the narrative to be "the Divine decree is true; human design is a lie." Surely, as Joseph himself says, "Solutions belong to God." Even if Joseph's dreams had the status of prophecy, God does not need man's help in fulfilling them. Perhaps the best answer to this question lies in Joseph's reason for naming his firstborn Menasseh. Joseph simply cannot face the psychic trauma of his sufferings at home in Canaan. Rabbi Jacob Mecklenberg goes beyond Rav Sa'adia Gaon in explaining Joseph's stated reason for the name Menasseh. He translates, "God removed the memory of all the suffering I endured in my father's house" (Commentary on *B'reishit* 41:51).[50]

Joseph then calls his second son Ephraim:

> כִּי הִפְרַנִי אֱ־לֹהִים בְּאֶרֶץ עָנְיִי
>
> For God made me fruitful in the land of my oppression. (*B'reishit* 41:52)

By contrast, he has no difficulty recalling his mercurial rise from slave to prince in Egypt itself.

But the Divine decree will not permit matters to so remain. The famine embraces not only Egypt, but also the Land of Canaan. When Joseph opens the storehouses and begins to sell grain to

50. הכתב והקבלה Avraham Yitzhak Friedman, ed. Vol. I (New York), 77–78.

a hungry population, word reaches Canaan that provisions are available in Egypt (*B'reishit* 42:1). Jacob instructs ten of his eleven remaining sons to travel to Egypt to make the requisite purchases. The eleventh son, Benjamin, the only remaining child of his beloved Rachel, is to remain with his father, lest any mishap befall him as it befell Joseph.

When the brothers arrive and stand before Joseph, he recognizes them immediately, but they have no inkling that they are standing before their long-lost brother. They are standing as mendicants before a powerful man who can either sell them needed foodstuffs or destroy them. Joseph remembers not only how abysmally his brothers treated him, but he also remembers his dreams of dominance, and he speaks harshly to them, accusing them of being spies. When they protest their good faith as mere buyers of grain who want only to return to Canaan with the sustenance needed to preserve themselves and their elderly father, Joseph persists in the attack. Under harsh scrutiny they reveal more of their circumstances. Originally they were twelve brothers, sons of one father. Their youngest brother remains with his father and another son is missing. Needless to say, they do not explain how that latter brother disappeared (*B'reishit* 42:1–20).

Joseph continues to bear down on them, insisting that one of them return to Canaan and bring back the remaining brother to prove their story. Joseph imprisons them all for three days, but then modifies his decree slightly. He tells the men that since he reveres God, he will allow the brothers to go free, but will take one of them hostage until Benjamin is brought to him.

The brothers now speak among themselves in Hebrew, unaware that the harsh ruler understands their every word. "We are surely being punished on account of our brother because we looked upon his anguish, yet paid no heed as he pleaded with us. That is why this trouble has come upon us." Reuben, the eldest brother, who had tried to save Joseph and restore him to his father, speaks up. "I told you not to sin against the boy, but you refused to listen. Now his blood is being avenged" (*B'reishit* 42:21–23). Joseph is now sufficiently moved that he turns away from them and weeps. But he is not yet ready to forgive.

The logical hostage to retain in Egypt would be the eldest brother, Reuben, but Reuben has just revealed that he was the one who wanted to save Joseph. As Ibn Ezra suggests, that is why Joseph selects Simeon, the second eldest, as hostage (*B'reishit* 42:24).

Without any other alternatives, the brothers saddle their animals, take the purchased provisions, and begin the journey back to Canaan. Meanwhile, surreptitiously, Joseph has the funds they brought for payment restored to them in their sacks of grain. While Joseph has not yet chosen to reveal his real relationship to them, he is not going to take money from his family. But his brothers clearly don't know this and it all terrifies them further.

Back in Canaan, they recount the harsh treatment they received from Egypt's ruler and how Simeon is being held hostage until Benjamin is brought down to prove the truthfulness of their account of themselves (*B'reishit* 42:14–25).

Jacob is distraught. "You have bereaved me! Joseph is gone, and now Simeon is gone. You want to take away Benjamin. All [these troubles] are upon me" (*B'reishit* 42:36–37). Anxious to return to Egypt with Benjamin and secure Simeon's release, Reuben, in desperation, says, "You can kill my two sons if I don't bring [Benjamin] back to you. Place him into my hands and I will bring him back to you" (*B'reishit* 42:36).

But Reuben's pleas fall on deaf ears. What consolation would Jacob have in killing his own grandchildren to avenge the loss of two sons? Rashi fills in the blanks in understanding Jacob's motivation in his adamant refusal. He would have thought, "My firstborn is an utter fool. Are his sons not my sons as well?" (Commentary on *B'reishit* 42:38). Jacob refuses to send the last remaining son of his beloved Rachel.

But the famine continues its brutal course and the purchased foodstuffs are exhausted. Jacob again instructs his sons to return to Egypt to purchase provisions. Judah now reminds his father that without Benjamin such a mission would, at best, be futile. Speaking for all of the brothers, Judah refuses unless Benjamin comes with them. There is an explosion of recrimination from Jacob. "You caused this trouble for me by gratuitously telling this man about the existence of another brother" (*B'reishit* 43:1–6). But, as the brothers respond, the inquiries of the ruler left them no choice. In any case, how could they have predicted the ruler's demand? (*B'reishit* 43:7).

Judah now gives his pledge. "Send the boy with me. Let us go so that we and our children can live rather than die. I shall be security for him. Hold me to account. If I do not bring him back to you and present him to you, I will stand guilty forever" (*B'reishit* 43:8–9).

Whereas Reuben's desperate plea fell upon deaf ears, Judah's words are now reluctantly accepted. The situation is now more desperate. More to the point, Judah's tone is more reassuring. He does not speak impulsively about Jacob killing his own grandchildren as payment for Benjamin's possible disappearance on the trip. It is Judah, who we know to have hatched the plot to sell Joseph into slavery, who stands up as the responsible adult worthy of trust.

In the Talmud, Judah's statement, "I will be security for him. You can hold me responsible," is turned into the prooftext for the law of the co-signer on a bill of indebtedness (*Bava Batra* 173b). In Halakha (and undoubtedly, in legal systems generally), if the borrower defaults on the loan and there is no collateral to be seized, the co-signer can be held liable. Judah is then telling Jacob, "I am the co-signer for my brother."

In a family torn apart by fratricidal hatred, Judah now articulates the principle that should govern the family of Israel. Each Israelite is supposed to be a co-signer for his brother. Neither Jacob nor his sons can guess at this point that the implacably harsh ruler in Egypt is, in fact, Joseph. When Joseph recovers the ability to face the demons of his past, and when he too can become a co-signer for his family, the drama will be brought to resolution. At that point, God will be revealed within the fabric of Joseph's dreams.

Chapter 25

All Israelites Are Bonded Together

PARASHAT VAYIGASH

THE SONS OF JACOB ARE SENT to Egypt a second time to purchase foodstuffs, and this time, Benjamin is with them. Before their departure, Jacob, who is filled with trepidation as he sends Benjamin, "for adversity lurks in the place of danger" (Commentary of Rashi on *B'reishit* 42:4), blesses his sons with the following words:

> וְאֵ־ל שַׁ־דַּי יִתֵּן לָכֶם רַחֲמִים לִפְנֵי הָאִישׁ וְשִׁלַּח לָכֶם אֶת אֲחִיכֶם אַחֵר וְאֶת בִּנְיָמִין וַאֲנִי כַּאֲשֶׁר שָׁכֹלְתִּי שָׁכָלְתִּי
>
> May E-l Sha-dai grant you mercy in the man's presence and may he send you and your *other brother* together with Benjamin [back home]. But if I am to be bereaved then so be it. (*B'reishit* 43:14)

There are two items in this prayer that are especially noteworthy. As pointed out earlier in *B'reishit*, to this point, the Divine name Sha-dai has been exclusively used in the context of the blessing of future progeny. Here, Jacob is praying for the safety of his progeny as they travel to Egypt. Furthermore, he prays for the return of "your other brother," which is curiously non-specific in its designation. The conscious reference has to be Simeon, who is being held hostage in Egypt. But the lack of specificity allows us to apply this reference to Joseph, who we, as the readers, know to be alive and, in fact, the feared ruler in Egypt. Perhaps Jacob himself was subconsciously hoping for the long lost Joseph (See Rashi on *B'reishit* 43:13).

When the brothers arrive in Egypt and stand in Joseph's presence with Benjamin, Joseph orders that they be brought to his house where a feast is to be prepared. This strange program of their all-powerful host fills the brothers with apprehension. They imagine that they will be set upon because of the initial purchase funds that were returned to them in their sacks instead of being taken for payment of the foodstuffs they had purchased. But Joseph's factotum reassures them that his master received the appropriate payment and all is in order. Simeon is brought to the house and finally their host arrives. He asks about their father Jacob and whether he is still alive. Then he lays his eyes upon Benjamin and blesses him, and, overwhelmed with emotion, he turns from them and weeps. For a second time, a meeting with his estranged and unwitting brothers has brought him to tears. But he recovers his composure, washes his face, and returns to the room. To the amazement of the brothers, he seats them exactly according to their birth order. He gives each brother a gift and five times the gift is given to Benjamin. Perhaps he is recalling how his father privileged him with a gift of the fine cloak not given to any other of his sons. It is important to note that the brothers do not react to this favoritism (See commentary of Seforno 43:34 and *B'reishit* 43:14–34).

The continuing sequence of events in this narrative is well known. The brothers take their sacks of foodstuff for the trip home. Unbeknown to them, the purchase funds have once more been replaced in their sacks but, in addition, Joseph's cup has been planted in Benjamin's sack. After they set out, soldiers are dispatched to apprehend them and one by one their sacks are searched. The purchase funds are discovered and finally the cup is found where it has been placed – in Benjamin's sack (*B'reishit* 44:1–12).

Just before the search began, the brothers had protested their innocence. "After all, we brought back the original funds from Canaan. Why would we steal silver or gold from your master's house? Whoever of your servants is found [with the cup] let him die and the rest of us will be slaves to the master" (*B'reishit* 44:8–9).

Now the horrified, grief stricken brothers tear their clothes in despair and they are brought back to Joseph's house. Judah, who had taken personal responsibility for Benjamin's safety, speaks up as the brothers' interlocutor. He renounces all claims to innocence but says, "God has exposed the sin of your servants." He modifies the original sentence uttered by the brothers before the search in a desperate attempt to both save Benjamin from possible death and to save the rest from the horror of facing their father without Benjamin. "We shall be slaves to my master, all of us, as well as the one in whose possession the cup was found" (*B'reishit* 44:16).

But Joseph will have none of it. "The one in whose possession the cup was found will become my slave, as for the rest of you, go in peace to your father" (*B'reishit* 44:17).

Now, in the longest speech of any person in *B'reishit*, Judah pleads for Benjamin's release. He recalls that only the forthright answers of the brothers to Joseph's original inquiries revealed Benjamin's existence. Only Joseph's insistence caused them to bring Benjamin to Egypt. At the time, the brothers explained how Benjamin's separation from their father could cause Jacob to die, but it was Joseph's demands that compelled them to bring Benjamin in any case. Jacob's most beloved wife Rachel had borne him but one other child apart from Benjamin and that child had disappeared. Their father's hold on life was tied totally to Benjamin. He had explicitly said, "If you take him from before me and anything happens to him, you will bring my white hair in anguish to the grave." Judah now tells the ruler that he bonded himself as security for his brother's safety, and if he now returns without him, he will bear total blame. Judah, who had once schemed to sell his brother Joseph into slavery and without regard for the anguish he would cause his father, now offers to take his brother Benjamin's place as a slave. Rashi reads into Judah's offer an assurance to Joseph that he would be a far more worthwhile slave to Joseph than Benjamin (Comments on *B'reishit* 44:33).

But more to the point, Judah, who had once been prepared to

do away with one brother, is now prepared to give his life for Benjamin (*B'reishit* 44:18–34). For the third time, Joseph breaks down in weeping and demands that everyone, apart from the brothers, leave the room. He turns to the shocked men and says, "I am Joseph. Does my father yet live?" (*B'reishit* 45:1–3). He had already been informed that Jacob lived, but at this point, he speaks no longer as the cold distant ruler, but rather as Israel's son. His query bears the mark of a man reborn to the family from which he had so violently been torn.

It is in that spirit that Joseph assures his brothers that he can no longer bear them ill will. Suddenly the full meaning of his original dreams becomes clear. Solutions after all belong not to man but to God. The brothers may have once schemed to destroy him, but God's plan was altogether different. Joseph was sent to Egypt for life. He knows that there will be five more years of famine. By forging Joseph's ascent to ruler in Egypt, God had fashioned the conditions under which his family can be saved from destruction. He tells his brothers that the family of Israel must descend to Egypt to live under his protection and solicitude. He says, "Hurry and go to my father and tell him, 'This is what your son Joseph says. God has placed me as ruler over all of Egypt. Come down to me; don't delay'" (*B'reishit* 45:9). Joseph kisses each brother, and they speak to each other as a family in which each brother cares for the other. With the Pharaoh's approval, elaborate gifts are sent back to Jacob with clear plans to have the family settle in the Land of Goshen close to Joseph. Joseph, who had so enraged his brothers when Jacob bestowed upon him his special garments, provides changes of clothes for each brother. Perhaps these changes of clothes are to be in place of the garments the brothers had torn when Joseph's cup was discovered in Benjamin's sack (Hizkuni on *B'reishit* 45:22). But to Benjamin he gives multiple changes of clothes and three hundred pieces of silver.

When the men first tell their father Jacob that Joseph is alive and waiting for his arrival in Egypt, his heart skips a beat and he cannot believe the news. But when he sees the wagons dispatched to bring him there, he is enabled to believe it and the joyous news revivifies his spirit. In the Torah's narrative, the name Jacob temporarily disappears, replaced by the name Israel. "Israel said, 'Enough! Joseph still lives. I will go to see him before I die'" (*B'reishit* 45:28). Ramban explains the alternation in the uses of the two names as reflective of Jacob's state of being. When Jacob is triumphant, he is designated as Israel and the news of Joseph renders his spirit triumphant. The absence of such triumph is expressed in the use of the name Jacob (Notes on *B'reishit* 46:2). Rabbi Meir Simkha HaKohen, in his *Meshekh Hokhma* adds to this by noting that when "Israel" is used, it refers to Jacob as the embodiment of the nation. In the Joseph narrative up to this point, the name Israel is used with reference to his children – the "Children of Israel" – and as Jacob's proper name only in his fateful interactions with Joseph and Judah. In the future history of Israel, the nation will be divided between two sovereignties: the kingdom of Israel and the kingdom of Judah under the Davidic dynasty.[51] This helps explain the use of the name Israel when Jacob tells Joseph to go to his brothers in Shechem and when he speaks to Judah before the second journey to Egypt. The rivalry of these two brothers is a signpost to the future rivalry of the two sovereignties and the tragedy of division, civil war, and exile.

The final reconciliation of the Davidic dynasty of Judah with tribes led by the progeny of Joseph will become a major part of the Messianic vision of ultimate redemption (Cf. Ezekiel 37:16). When Jacob is convinced that Joseph still lives, he personifies a nation in its completeness with all the tribes of Israel finally reconciled.

When the journey to Egypt begins, Jacob and his family first go to Beersheva where Jacob initially began his journey to Haran. Beersheva is also the place at which Jacob's father Isaac was forewarned by God not to descend to Egypt even in the face of famine (*B'reishit* 26:2–5). But now Jacob is preparing precisely such a move. Thus he goes to Beersheva to "offer sacrifices to the God of his father Isaac" (*B'reishit* 46:1). He is seeking the Divine imprimatur for his descent to Egypt. God consents to his move, telling Jacob not to be afraid (*B'reishit* 46:2–4, Seforno on 45:28).

51. Rabbi Meir Simkha HaKohen, משך חכמה (Eshkol), 30.

There is no sense in telling anyone not to be afraid unless there is a reason for alarm. Here we must attend to the subtlety in the text.

> וַיֹּאמֶר אֱ־לֹהִים לְיִשְׂרָאֵל בְּמַרְאֹת הַלַּיְלָה וַיֹּאמֶר יַעֲקֹב יַעֲקֹב וַיֹּאמֶר הִנֵּנִי. וַיֹּאמֶר אָנֹכִי הָאֵ־ל אֱ־לֹהֵי אָבִיךָ אַל תִּירָא מֵרְדָה מִצְרַיְמָה כִּי לְגוֹי גָּדוֹל אֲשִׂימְךָ שָׁם. אָנֹכִי אֵרֵד עִמְּךָ מִצְרַיְמָה וְאָנֹכִי אַעַלְךָ גַם עָלֹה וְיוֹסֵף יָשִׁית יָדוֹ עַל עֵינֶיךָ.
>
> E-lohim spoke to Israel in the visions of the night saying, 'Jacob, Jacob' and [Jacob] said 'I am here.' [God] said, 'I am God, the God of your father. Fear not the descent to Egypt, for I will make you a great nation there. I shall descend with you and then I will allow you to return ascendantly. Joseph's hand will close your eyes. (*B'reishit* 46:2–4)

We should first note that God is not denoted here by the Tetragramaton, but by the relatively impersonal E-lohim. While He reveals Himself to "Israel in the visions of the night," He addresses him only as "Jacob." Jacob is told that in the alien and therefore alarming Land of Egypt, he should not fear, because Egypt is designated as the place where Jacob's family will become the "great nation" that Abraham was told would issue from his loins (*B'reishit* 12:2). Now in the vision accompanying the enactment of the Covenant Between the Parts, Abraham was overcome with "great, dark dread." He was told that three generations would be enslaved in a place of exile, but that the fourth generation would go free and return to the Promised Land (*B'reishit* 15:7–16). That process will begin with Jacob's descent to Egypt. All of this is revealed in Israel's "visions of the night" that parallels Abraham's "great, dark dread." In the context of that vision, Jacob, rather than Israel, is addressed, for in Egyptian slavery there can be no triumphant spirit. This is the last explicit revelation that Jacob will receive from God. God's presence will be seemingly eclipsed as Jacob and his children descend into exile. But God will not abandon Israel. His Presence, though undetected, will descend into exile with Jacob and ascend with Israel at the time of redemption.

At the point of descent into Egypt, the Torah provides a complete list of Jacob's children and children's children, organized in descending numbers according to their mothers: first the 33 descendants of Leah, then the 16 descendants of Zilpah, next the 14 descendants of Rachel, and finally the 7 descendants of Bilhah. The numbers create a pattern with Zilpah, Leah's maidservant having just half of the count of Leah's children minus one, and Bilhah, Rachel's maidservant, having exactly half the count of Rachel's children. However, if one adds the names of Leah's descendants entering Egypt, the number only comes to 32. How are we to account for this discrepancy? The commentaries offer different solutions, and the most convincing answer is provided by Ibn Ezra. Jacob himself is to be counted in the initial number, and with Jacob added, the final count of the House of Israel now corresponds to the number 70 reported by the Torah (*B'reishit* 46:8–47; Commentary of Ibn Ezra on 46:27). There is a very different, curious resolution found in the *Da'at Zekenim Mi Ba'alei Tos'fot.*[52] "When they descended to Egypt, the Holy One, Blessed be He, Himself in His glory, was counted with them, for if you count those listed, there are only 69, and Scripture says '70 persons.' Thus God was counted and the number rises to 70." Here it is proposed that the missing "person" is the Presence of God. This has the advantage of attaching the census to the promise of God descending and ascending with them, as stated in Israel's "visions of the night."

The family of Israel arrives. Joseph comes to greet them in his chariot and then falls upon his father's neck with an abundance of tears. The reunion is complete and the House of Israel is made whole (*B'reishit* 46:29–30).

52. מקראות גדולות - בראשית, ad locum (Tanach Publishing Company, 1959).

Chapter 26

Jacob Our Father Did Not Die

PARASHAT VAYEHI

THE BOOK OF *B'REISHIT* ENDS with accounts of the death and burial of Jacob and the last days of Joseph. In the very last verse of Parashat VaYigash, the Torah says, "Israel dwelled in the Land of Egypt in the Land of Goshen. They settled there and greatly multiplied" (*B'reishit* 47:27). Clearly the designation "Israel" here refers not simply to Jacob the individual, but to the people that emerge from this loins. The sages begin the next and last Parasha of this book, *Vayehi*, with a verse that is in the middle of the same *piska*, or paragraph unit in the text. This unusual way of breaking between *parshiot* can easily obscure the connection and contrast between the last verse of *Vayigash* and the first verse of *Vayehi*. In contrast to the *Vayigash* verse, the subject of the next verse is Jacob the individual. Here his proper name is given as Jacob and we are told how many years Jacob lived in Egypt and his age when he died (*B'reishit* 48:28). Immediately after that, the Torah says, "the time of Israel's death drew near and he called his son Joseph saying to him . . . do not bury me in Egypt" (*B'reishit* 48:29).

If we follow the commentary of *Meshekh Hokhma* cited in the previous chapter, the change in this verse from the name Jacob to the name Israel, now used as a personal designation, indicates that the place of Jacob's burial is of paramount importance to the nation. While Jacob's children and grandchildren are enjoying wondrous success and great fecundity in Egypt, they will attain their destiny only in the Land where their progenitors are buried.

The Patriarch Israel instructs Joseph, a ruler in Egypt after all, with the power and authority to attend to his wishes, to bury him appropriately in the gravesite of Machpelah in Hebron together with his parents, his grandparents, and his wife Leah. He extracts an oath from Joseph and to formalize that oath he says, "Place your hand under my thigh" (*B'reishit* 47:29–30). As we already saw with Abraham, "under my thigh" is a euphemism for placing the hand upon Jacob's genitals, and in Midrashic tradition, more specifically upon the mark of the Covenant of Circumcision. Now in Abraham's case, the servant was being asked to swear that he would bring back to Canaan only an appropriate wife for Isaac. Here, Joseph is being instructed to swear that he would not bury his father in Egypt, but in the gravesite in Hebron.

In the earlier case of Abraham, the meaning of what seems to us to be a bizarre act is this. In fulfilling his vow and bringing back an appropriate wife, the servant is ensuring the continuity of Abraham's family and, for this reason, swears upon the organ of generation and the sign of the covenant that consecrates Abraham's procreative future to an eternal covenant with God. However, here we are not dealing with procreation, but with death and burial. The burial site of the progenitors of Israel is destined to become a magnet for future generations, cementing the bond between past and future. The tomb of Israel's ancestors will become the womb of the nation, and the covenant of circumcision and all that it means for Israel will thus continue from generation to generation.

Presumably, it is this that explains the form of the oath. The oath is taken, and "Israel prostrates himself at the head of the bed" (*B'reishit* 47:31). With this, the *piska* that overlaps *Parashat Vayigash* and *Parashat Veyehi* concludes.

In the next textual unit, upon hearing that his father's health is failing, Joseph takes his two sons Manasseh and Ephraim to Jacob's bedside. The Torah says, "They tell *Jacob*, 'Your son, Joseph, is coming to see you.' *Israel* summoned his strength and sat up in bed" (*B'reishit* 48:2). In other words, the enfeebled Jacob summons all of his power to speak as Israel, the Patriarch of his people. He recalls his journey to Luz-Bethel when he first returned home from Haran. There God said to him, "Your name was Jacob," and then confirmed the bestowal of the new name Israel upon him (*B'reishit* 35:9–10). The ensuing conversation closely paraphrases God's revealed words to him and His blessing. Just as the name Jacob is used in the original account in *Parashat Vishlakh* where this revelation occurred, so too does the Torah here use the name Jacob.

> וַיֹּאמֶר יַעֲקֹב אֶל יוֹסֵף אֵ־ל שַׁ־דַּי נִרְאָה אֵלַי בְּלוּז בְּאֶרֶץ כְּנָעַן וַיְבָרֶךְ אֹתִי. וַיֹּאמֶר אֵלַי הִנְנִי מַפְרְךָ וְהִרְבִּיתִךָ וּנְתַתִּיךָ לִקְהַל עַמִּים וְנָתַתִּי אֶת הָאָרֶץ הַזֹּאת לְזַרְעֲךָ אַחֲרֶיךָ אֲחֻזַּת עוֹלָם.
>
> Jacob said to Joseph, E-l Sha-dai appeared to me in Luz in the Land of Canaan and blessed me. He said to me, "I will make you fruitful and increase you making you an *assembly of peoples* and giving this land to your descendants as an eternal inheritance." (*B'reishit* 48:3–4)

Jacob then tells his son, "Ephraim and Menasseh will be as Reuben and Simeon to me" (*B'reishit* 48:5). Joseph, the firstborn to his mother Rachel, though not of his father, is assigned two portions in the tribal allotment of Israel emerging out of Jacob's loins. Once again, the right of primogeniture is being shifted to a younger child, in this case, Joseph.

Jacob now continues the conversation. "Alas, when I came from Padan, Rachel, to my sorrow, died in the Land of Canaan on the journey, at some distance from Ephrat. I buried her on the road to Ephrat which is Bethlehem" (*B'reishit* 48:7).

Rashi, Ibn Ezra, Radak, and Ramban understand this statement as Jacob's rationalization before Joseph for not having buried Rachel in the Machpelah gravesite where he, himself is to be buried. But especially convincing are Professor Nahum Sarna's comments that what Jacob is really doing is bemoaning Rachel's early death, which prevented her from having more children and serving as a progenitor of multiple tribes in Israel.[53] The assignment of one more tribal portion to her descendants through Ephraim and Menasseh serves to memorialize her and

53. JPS Commentary, 326.

to give substance to God's promise before her death while giving birth to Benjamin that "an assembly of peoples" will yet emerge. Jacob is determining that Benjamin, Ephraim, and Menasseh will constitute that assembly (See Rashi on *B'reishit* 35:11, 48:4). The Torah now says, "Israel sees Joseph's children and he says, 'Who are they?'" (*B'reishit* 48:8). As we will be presently told, Jacob's eyes have grown dim with age so that he cannot see his grandsons clearly (*B'reishit* 48:10). Joseph responds, "They are my sons that God has given to me here" (*B'reishit* 48:9). Jacob asks him to bring them close so that he might bless them, and he hugs them and kisses them.

Just as Isaac became blind and could not see the son he was to bless, so too is Jacob blind and unable to see his grandsons. Just as Isaac had kissed Jacob before he blessed him, so does Jacob now kiss Ephraim and Menasseh. Joseph carefully sets his firstborn son, Menasseh, adjacent to Jacob's right hand to receive the primacy in the blessing and Ephraim at Jacob's left. But Jacob crisscrosses his hands, placing his right on Ephraim's head and his left Menasseh's. When Joseph sees this, he assumes that Jacob's blindness is preventing him from seeing that he has mistakenly placed his right hand on Ephraim. He attempts to switch Jacob's hands, and says, "That is not right, father. The firstborn is over here. Place your right hand on his head" (*B'reishit* 48:13–18).

Now when Jacob crisscrosses his hands, the Torah says,

> שִׂכֵּל אֶת יָדָיו כִּי מְנַשֶּׁה הַבְּכוֹר
>
> He redirected his hand even though Menasseh was the firstborn. (*B'reishit* 48:14)

The verb שִׂכֵּל – *sikel* (as in *sekhel*) is translated by Targum Onkeles as אחכימינון – *akhkiminun*, or "directed with intentionality." In response to Joseph, Jacob says, "I know, my son, I know. [Menasseh] will also be a people and be great, but his younger brother will be greater than he" (*B'reishit* 18:19). In other words, "My actions are not a consequence of blindness. I am consciously assigning primacy to the younger son."

When the blind Isaac gave his primacy blessing to the younger son Jacob, he had been tricked and did so unwittingly. But the equally blind Jacob tells Joseph that he is not making a mistake. In willfully granting his own blessing to the younger Ephraim, Jacob is affirming the legitimacy of transferring primogeniture to a younger child. He is affirming the legitimacy of his own claims to the birthright against the claims of Essau once again.

It is striking that while the Torah will later canonize the claims of the firstborn to primogeniture and a double portion in the estate of his father, even if the firstborn is not born to a favored wife, with the patriarchs it is different (*Devarim* 21:17). Abraham's true heir, Isaac, is his second son. Isaac's true heir is his second son, Jacob. Jacob assigns the firstborn's double portion in his patrimony to Joseph, the son of his beloved Rachel, and then assigns primacy to Joseph's second son Ephraim. There is something else strikingly noteworthy in the life of the patriarchs and their wives. Isaac is born to a postmenopausal Sarah, who was barren during her natural childbearing years. Rebecca is initially barren until Isaac's prayer for children became almost desperate (*B'reishit* 25:21 and Rashi's commentary ad locum). Rachel, Joseph's mother, was initially barren. Both in the shift of primogeniture and in the manner of the production of children, the Torah is portraying the emergence of the "great nation" that was promised to Abraham as creation against the natural order of things. The fruitfulness of Jacob's descendants stands in contrast to the emergence of Israel during the patriarchal period.

With Jacob's death, the patriarchal period draws to a close. Before his death, Jacob gathers his sons around him and tells them what will occur to them at the "end of days" (*B'reishit* 49:1). The *Da'at Zekenim* is certainly correct in understanding this "end of days" to mean what will happen to the tribes "after the 430 years" and the return of the fourth generation to the Promised Land, as promised to Abraham in the Covenant Between the Parts (*B'reishit* 15:7–9). The context of Jacob's oracular testament reveals the bare outlines of the future history of the tribes of Israel.

After Jacob is dead and buried, the brothers become apprehensive. Perhaps Joseph will recall how brutally he was treated by his brothers when they cast him in a pit and were prepared to sell him into slavery. Again Joseph reiterates that, far from bearing them ill will, he sees himself as God's messenger divinely sent to Egypt to prepare the way for life and blessing. Joseph fully internalizes the prophecies given to Abraham, Isaac, and Jacob and that a time will yet come in which a strong and populous people will be redeemed from Egypt and proceed to the land of the fathers.[54] Joseph, second-in-command in Egypt, married to the daughter of the priest of On, fully at home and secure in the power structure of Egypt, casts his lot with his family. Just as Jacob had Joseph promise that he would not bury him in Egypt, so too does Joseph extract an oath from the Israelites: "When God takes notice of you, you are to take my remains with you from this land to the land that He promised to Abraham, Isaac, and Jacob" (*B'reishit* 50:24). When Joseph dies, his body is embalmed as Jacob's body was embalmed, according to standard Egyptian practice (*B'reishit* 50:20–26). Joseph's remains are placed in a coffin, but the coffin is not buried. Using different words, Joseph repeats the Divine promise Jacob was given in the visions of the night in Beersheva before he left the Land of Canaan for the Land of Egypt. "God will take notice of you and take you ascendantly from this land to the land he swore to Abraham, Isaac, and Jacob" (*B'reishit* 50:24).

At the time of the redemption, Moses will be told to repeat those very words to the elders of Israel: "I have taken notice of you" (*Sh'mot* 3:16). The ultimate, successfully assimilated Israelite, Joseph, has coined the very phrase that will signal the beginning of Israel's return to her Land. Moses will not depart from Egypt until he locates and takes Joseph's remains with him (*Sh'mot* 13:19). The patriarchs of Israel will be revivified in the "great nation" promised from the beginning to Abraham.

> Rabbi Yitshak said to Rav Nahman: "Rabbi Yohanan said: 'Jacob our father did not die.' Rav Nahman retorted: 'Was it then for naught that eulogies were intoned, the embalmers embalmed his body, the gravediggers dug his grave?' Rabbi

54. חברת תנ"ך edition of the מקראות גדולות, 617.

Yitshak explained: 'I am expounding a scriptural verse: 'You my servant Jacob, do not fear!' says God. 'Do not tremble, Israel, for I shall redeem you from afar and your children from the land of their captivity.' (Jeremiah 30:10) This verse identifies Jacob with his children. Just as his children live, so does he live." (*Ta'anit* 5b)